THE LITTLE HISTORY OF SWANSEA

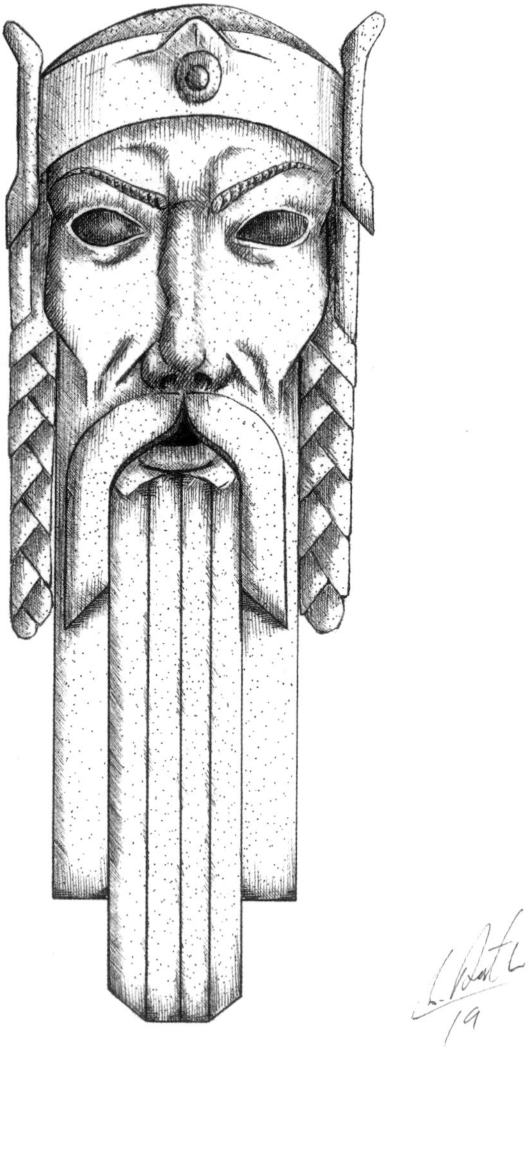

THE LITTLE HISTORY OF SWANSEA

DAVID GWYNN

The History Press

First published 2020

The History Press
97 St George's Place, Cheltenham,
Gloucestershire, GL50 3QB
www.thehistorypress.co.uk

British Library Cataloguing in Publication Data.
A catalogue record for this book is available from the British Library.

ISBN 978 0 7509 9307 4

Typesetting and origination by The History Press
Printed and bound in Great Britain by TJ International Ltd.

CONTENTS

PREFACE

SWANSEA JACK

Before I launch into the detail of Swansea's history, I would like to recall a story of bravery and heroism that has Swansea folk brimming with pride. It is the story of a dog. A black dog. He was a retriever, with a longish, slightly curly black coat, and he lived in the general area of the North Dock with his owner, a chap called William Thomas. Jack had briefly been owned by another man, but had disgraced himself by killing some ducks in Parc Llewellyn. Not an auspicious start for a hero. A new home was needed for Jack.

He found that with William Thomas. It is thought that Jack, for a dog living near the docks, was actually afraid of water, but his owner encouraged him to go swimming in the dock with some local boys. During the play they had, Jack would happily drag boys by their belts, or if they had a shirt on, their collars, to the side of the dock.

In June 1931, when Jack was just 9 months old, a 12-year-old boy got into a scuffle on the dockside and fell in. As he got into trouble, Jack jumped in, grabbed him and brought him to the side. A few weeks later, he rescued a swimmer from the river near the West Pier. This brought him to the attention of the press, and the Swansea Corporation awarded him a silver collar. By August 1934, he had rescued fourteen people, and his fame was spreading. In 1936 he had the 'Bravest Dog of the Year' title given to him by the *Star* newspaper.

His exploits also earned him a silver cup from the Lord Mayor of London, and he received two bronze medals – also dubbed the canine VC – from the National Canine Defence League; a unique achievement. The legend says that he rescued twenty-seven people from either the river or the docks at Swansea. Some say twenty-nine, but he also rescued another dog from the water and a sack of puppies, so that might explain the discrepancy.

He was still a young dog when, in 1937, he ingested some rat poison and died. There have been conspiracy theories that this was done on purpose by some rogue, but the docks would have been plagued by rats and, as a consequence, rat poison would have been put down to kill them. It was probably just unfortunate that Jack managed to eat something that had been laced with poison.

His legacy, however, lives on. Today, Swansea people are nicknamed 'Jacks', and the supporters of Swansea City Football Club have been dubbed the 'Jack Army'. A memorial, paid for by public subscription, stands on the Promenade near the St Helen's Cricket Ground.

Now, let's turn to the history and development of the town and its people – the Jacks of Swansea.

East view of Swansea Castle, 1740, by Samuel and Nathaniel Buck.

INTRODUCTION

Swansea did not exist before the arrival of the Normans, around the turn of the eleventh and twelfth centuries. The area that was to become the town was, more than likely, just desolate riverbank occupied by a few birds and maybe some wild Welsh ponies. There is hardly any evidence to suggest that early man created anything permanent on the riverside acres that became Swansea. A few odd axe heads, flint tools and arrow heads have turned up, but they do not suggest permanent populations on the site. Of course, anything that might have existed would have long since been destroyed as the town grew, but it would seem that the early settlers in the area did not find the site particularly appealing. To find out who lived in these parts in earlier times, we must look for evidence in nearby Gower.

Today, Gower, Oystermouth and parts of the former Lliw Valley are incorporated into the City and County of Swansea. It is a unitary authority created in 1996. A previous local government reorganisation in 1974 had brought peninsular Gower into Swansea's domain – the Gower Rural District Council had been in charge there up until then. Oystermouth Urban District Council, which included Mumbles, had been absorbed by Swansea in 1920. Lliw Valley was brought into existence in 1974 and, along with Swansea, Neath and Afan (Port Talbot), formed West

Glamorgan. Lliw Valley covered Gorseinon, Pontardulais and the Upper Swansea Valley. All this disappeared again in 1996 when West Glamorgan was dissolved as a county council, and the area was divided into the City and County of Swansea and the County Borough of Neath Port Talbot. Swansea had been created a city in 1969 to celebrate the investiture of the Prince of Wales. It maintained its city status through all the subsequent changes that were made to local government in Wales.

In this book, I will endeavour to relate the history of Swansea as it existed prior to the 1974 reorganisation. I will refer to Gower occasionally, but a proper history of the peninsula will require another book.

1

EARLIEST TIMES TO THE COMING OF THE NORMANS

IN THE BEGINNING

Whilst the riverside site now occupied by Swansea was, it seems, largely ignored by early man, the same cannot be said of peninsular Gower. The first evidence of human activity in the area comes from Rhosili in the form of a 75,000-year-old hand axe. Elsewhere in Wales, there is evidence of human activity from 250,000 years ago, but it only suggests nomadic groups passing through rather than permanent settlements. At this time, there was no Bristol Channel, and a large plain linked Wales with the south-west of England, Ireland and mainland Europe. Human beings could walk to these parts and clearly did so at this time.

In order to make the understanding of history easier, the passage of time has been conveniently divided into 'ages'. So, we have the Stone Age, itself divided into the Old Stone Age (Palaeolithic), the Middle Stone Age (Mesolithic) and the New Stone Age (Neolithic). These were followed by the Bronze Age and then the Iron Age.

In Gower, artefacts have been found at sites from all of these periods. From the Old Stone Age comes the skeleton of a young man found in Paviland Cave on the south Gower coast. Uncovered in the early nineteenth century and studied initially by William Buckland in 1823, it was originally thought to be that of a woman, 'The Red Lady of Paviland'. Later research declared it to be a young man, who had been buried in the cave, it is thought, with some ritual, 26,000 years ago. This cave is one of the most important archaeological sites in Wales. So many items have been discovered there that it has to be considered to be of national importance.

The ending of the Ice Age brought dramatic climate change with rising temperatures and rising sea levels. As the sea inundated the lower lying-land, so Britain became a wooded island, and as the New Stone Age dawned the population of these islands grew and began to settle. Burial sites of importance from this long age and into the Bronze Age can be found at King Arthur's Stone on Cefn Bryn in Gower; Giant's Grave at Llethrid Cwm in south Gower and Swine Houses (or Sweyne's Howes) on Rhosili Down. The number of Bronze Age cairns in the area indicate a growing population, but evidence of early domestic dwellings is scant. The most important comes from a site within the urban area of Swansea, at Coltshill, near Mumbles. An excavation of a Bronze Age cairn in 1969 produced pottery fragments, a hearth and the post holes of a dwelling.

The Iron Age was also, largely, the age of the Celts. Celtic peoples were on the move throughout Europe at this time, and where they settled they built enclosures, usually defended, that were fortresses in time of strife. In Gower, the most impressive of these is at Cil Ifor Top in Llanrhidian. Evidence has been found there for huts within the enclosure. Other Celtic enclosures have been identified at the Knave near Mewslade; Redley Cliff near Caswell; Pwll Ddu Head and in Bishopston Valley.

THE ROMAN OCCUPATION

From Roman sources, we learn that in South Wales there were two Celtic tribes at the end of the Iron Age. The Silures in the south-east, and the Demetae in the south-west. It seems that the border between them ran approximately through the Swansea and Gower area. This would not be a border in the sense that we would understand the term, but rather broad lands which would change hands from time to time, and where the two tribes mixed – either peaceably or in conflict. Roman sources suggest that the Silures were a warlike people whose warriors were determined and brave. It may well have taken the Romans some effort over a period of time to subdue them.

The Romans had subjugated the whole area by 74 CE. They quickly established forts at what, for them, were strategic points. Nidum, Leucarum and Maridunum – that is, Neath, Loughor and Carmarthen. These were all classed as auxiliary forts and would have been subject to the legionary fort that existed at Isca, which today is Caerleon. Both Isca and Maridunum had substantial urban centres, where the populations would have been drawn from local people. It has been suggested that the Loughor fort was constructed very early in the Roman occupation, probably around 74–75 CE. The Roman army left Wales around 393 CE.

Given 300 years of occupation, it is not surprising that many Roman artefacts have turned up throughout the area. Coins, both individually and in hoards, have been found. The remains of a Roman villa have been uncovered at Oystermouth, and pottery, weapons, jewellery and coins have been found in many of the caves of Gower, suggesting that they were occupied by the native Celts, either as residences or workshops. It has been suggested that there may have been several Roman or Romano-British estates in Gower, although there has been no evidence uncovered of buildings.

It seems that the native Celtic people carried on their lives much as before, tolerating the presence of the Roman occupiers. After initially resisting them, they eventually settled into their old ways, whilst enjoying the veneer of civilisation that contact with Rome brought. Trade could now be carried out with communities in most of Europe, the Middle East and North Africa. Those who became citizens of the Roman Empire were free to travel within the empire or, if not, also to fight and die for it if they joined Rome's army. Some, unhappily, became slaves and were transported forcibly to other parts of the empire.

It is very likely that the Romans built a road to link Leucarum with Nidum and Isca. Today, we can trace the possible route of this road, by following the B4620 out of Loughor and through Garden Village and on to Middle Road in Gendros and down to the River Tawe. On Stafford Common there is evidence of temporary practice camps, thrown up during the training of soldiers and then abandoned once their job was done. This coastal road has been dubbed the Via Julia Maritima by modern commentators, but its Roman title is unknown.

The crossing of the Tawe is an interesting puzzle. At this time, the river would have been much less of a barrier than it might seem. However, it was necessary to have a crossing, and we can only speculate as to whether there was a bridge at this point. Evidence uncovered in 1846 whilst the North Dock was being constructed suggests that the crossing was in fact a ford. In 1877 the Rev. J.D. Davies wrote the following description of the discovery of the ford by Colonel Grant Francis, who had been at the site at the time:

> In constructing the lock at the upper end of the North Dock ... a regularly formed paved crossing was discovered. This work was carefully constructed of strong timber, wattled on its upper and lower sides, while the road within was packed with three horizontal layers of good sized boulders, upon which were laid, from bank to bank of the river, squared blocks of native sandstone. This roadway was in sound condition, and undoubtedly ancient, for it lay several feet below the then existing bed of the Tawey. From its systematic and excellent construction, the engineers were of the opinion that it was of Roman workmanship.

If, indeed, this was a Roman ford across the Tawe, then it would have enabled soldiers, either on horseback or on foot, to cross the river in relative safety. Although there have been odd finds in and around the centre of Swansea, including a piece of a cooking pot, there is currently insufficient evidence to suggest there was any kind of settlement near the ford. The Romans would not have needed a fort here, as the forts at Loughor and Neath were near enough to provide assistance should it be needed. It is possible that a tavern of some kind might have been sited here, to provide rest and refreshment for travellers, but there was no settled community here.

A ford also crossed the Loughor Estuary, and may have been of similar construction to this one across the Tawe. The road would then have continued to Maridunum. It is also thought that a side road left the main road somewhere to the west of the Tawe and headed down to Oystermouth, where an estate, possibly of some importance, was centred on a villa. The remains of this villa lie in the churchyard at Oystermouth and were discovered before 1697 when Isaac Hamon of Bishopston described the small coloured tiles, or tesserae. Local superstition identified this tiled floor as the

'Saint's Pavement'. It may have been that the first church in Oystermouth was built amid the ruins of a Roman villa, possibly because if the local folk believed in the Saint's Pavement myth, it was thought a good idea to build the church on a site already felt to be holy.

All these discoveries and the discussions that have resulted lead to a picture of Roman South Wales that is quite bucolic. There are five forts at equal distances from each other (the fifth fort was called Bomium, but no one knows quite where that was sited, other than between Isca and Nidum). There were farming estates, each centred on a villa, although there is no evidence to show where these were. The local Celtic population continued to live in or near their hillforts, tolerating the presence of the Roman overlords and their army. The population could well have been quite cosmopolitan, as soldiers would come from anywhere in the empire, as would traders and craftsmen looking for opportunities to work.

Money, in the form of coins, was in general circulation, and was used by both the Roman community and the native population. The caves in the cliffs of South Gower were still being used for several purposes including homes, workshops and for burials. The sea would have provided fish and shellfish – and at Oystermouth, oysters were being picked from the beds that gave the village its name. Maybe the villa there was the home of an entrepreneur in the oyster industry? The oyster beds were certainly cared for, if not actually farmed in the modern sense. Society would have had a structure and generally, as a result, peace held sway.

Trouble, however, was brewing on the distant eastern borders of the Roman Empire. Incursions into the empire by Germanic tribes meant that military resources had to be allocated to those lands, and so the Roman army in Britain was gradually withdrawn to defend Rome herself. It seems that the entire military presence in Wales had gone by 393 CE.

THE DARK AGES

I make no apology for using the term 'the Dark Ages', although its use to describe the period between the end of Roman rule and the arrival of the Normans has declined in recent years. It is, however, a useful term to cover the period between 400 CE and about 1100 CE. Over the 700 years between these dates, very little archaeological evidence is to be found. The adoption of Christianity and the customs of that religion meant burials were not accompanied by grave goods. Very few coins have been found and very little pottery remains.

For the first 200 years or so after the Roman withdrawal, those who had enjoyed a degree of power and wealth during the latter days of empire continued to follow their established lifestyle. Some Roman settlements continued to be occupied, the roads laid out during the Roman period continued to be used, and indeed continue in use today. Latin remained in use until as late as 500 CE. Trade must have carried on, although probably at a lesser rate than previously. Evidence for this is to be found in the remains of pottery from Gaul and the eastern Mediterranean dating up to 650 CE.

This period, around the middle of the seventh century, saw the local population, who it seems were descended from the Demetae, beginning to establish a political and social order. Gower, including the area that became Swansea, straddled the border country between the land occupied by the Demetae and the land occupied by the Silures, the other South Walian tribe, and was often forced to shift allegiance. In around 650 CE it had its own king, named as Merchwyn ap Glywys. However, as time went on, Gower was absorbed into a larger kingdom which stretched from Gwent to the eastern edge of Dyfed. This was the kingdom of Glywysing, and was ruled over by Meurig ap Tewdrig and his descendants. Dyfed, to the west, comprised what is today Pembrokeshire, Carmarthenshire and parts of Cardiganshire. This kingdom was influenced by Irish settlers and possibly settlers from France.

By the tenth century, the political landscape had changed, and Gower became a disputed land. Dyfed was now largely the kingdom of Deheubarth and Glywysing had become Morgannwg, named for Morgan Hen who ruled there from about 934 to 974. From 958, Gower endured frequent attacks from Dyfed, and in 984 Einon of Dyfed, the grandson of Hywel Dda, was killed whilst making an attempt to add Gower to his realm. At some point, though, the men of Dyfed were successful, and Gower, the largest commote in Wales, along with the commotes of Carnwyllion (Llanelli) and Cydweli (Kidwelly) were merged into the cantref of Ystrad Tywi, and became part of Deheubarth.

All of South Wales had to contend with further disruption from the tenth century onwards, as its coastline was a target for the Vikings, seaborne raiders who had already established settlements in Ireland, on the Isle of Man and in the Highlands and islands of Scotland. The accepted view is that the Vikings just wanted to plunder, and consequently were not too concerned about the death and destruction that they caused. The truth is that they were just as concerned with creating settlements, trading and working hard to create wealth for themselves. A sizeable chunk of northern France had already been colonised and become Normandy, and from there the Normans, as these French Vikings became known, established kingdoms in Sicily and Naples. Perhaps they hoped to achieve the same in South Wales, but found the opposition much tougher to overcome.

WHAT'S IN A NAME?

Viking names appear all along the South Wales coast, from Skokholm in Pembrokeshire to Steepholm off Barry. And so we come to perhaps the biggest South Wales mystery to involve the Vikings – is Swansea a Viking place name? We know that the Welsh name for the city, 'Abertawe', simply means the mouth of the River Tawe. An alternative Welsh name, which appears occasionally in early Welsh writing, is 'Sein Henydd', the origin of which is much less clear. However, many words and much ink has been expended discussing the origin of the name 'Swansea'.

Before discussing the name of the town, we need to spend some time establishing whether there was any kind of settlement on the site before the arrival of the Normans. It has been argued that before the Normans arrived, the whole area was nothing more than 'a stretch of sand, the haunt of sea-gull and plover', to quote Sir John Lloyd. This, of course, begs the question, why would the Normans choose to build a castle on a desolate stretch of river bank with no obvious advantages?

The Romans had chosen to rule the area from a fort at Loughor and another at Neath. Apart from a ford across the lower part of the river, they largely ignored the Swansea area. The Normans, however, were attempting to conquer and subdue a much more sophisticated local population, with administrative structures and mores already well established. Also, they were aware that their castles had to be much more impregnable and using marshland and river as part of the defences made a great deal of sense. They were trying to conquer a Christian land, where the people worshipped the same god, in much the same way as they did. Perhaps a castle on a previously unoccupied site would have meant greater acceptance by local people.

The additional factor that we are only able to speculate about is whether or not there was a community – perhaps religious or maybe secular – on the site before the Normans arrived. Some evidence suggests that there was something there. Excavations in the early twentieth century found skeletons in quantity below Worcester Place, where the edge of the mound of Swansea's first castle would have been. Could this suggest that a religious community of some kind existed there, or at least that there had been a church and a small settlement there?

An early Welsh name that has been associated with Swansea by scholars is 'Lanngemei' and Colonel Llewellyn Morgan suggested, having become convinced himself, that this was the name of an early Celtic foundation, in or very near Swansea, that the Normans ripped down and built their castle over.

An 1838 view of Swansea Castle, by Newman & Co.

If the Vikings had established some sort of settlement on the site, then it would have been destined to struggle for survival in tumultuous times. There was great rivalry between Deheubarth and Morgannwg, with Gower placed between them. It is frequently asserted that the name Swansea derives from the Viking name 'Sweyn' with the addition of 'eie' meaning 'reach', or arguably 'island'.

There is no island at the mouth of the Tawe, other than a mudbank that appears at certain times when there is a low tide. It probably was never, nor has ever been, named. 'Sweyn', however, could refer to King Sweyn Forkbeard, who was the father of King Canute, was King of Denmark, had briefly been King of England himself, and was known as a sea rover. Perhaps the Vikings had established a temporary mooring for their ships at the mouth of the River Tawe and chose to call it 'Sweyn's eie'; or Sweyn himself had created a temporary base from which to operate. Another suggestion is that Sweyn was shipwrecked on this stretch of the Welsh coast. Why the name has survived is a mystery but it did and has been used in many forms from the twelfth century to the present day.

2

NORMANS TO THE END OF THE STUARTS

THE NORMANS SETTLE IN

Whatever the reason or reasons that convinced the Normans that here was a good spot to build their first castle, it was of their normal motte-and-bailey type. The man responsible for this was Henry de Newburgh, Earl of Warwick. Until 1106 the Welsh commote of Gwyr was held by Hywel ap Goronwy, and it was his death in that year that led Henry I, King of England, to invest the commote in de Newburgh, as part of a wider scheme to ensure that the lands in Wales came into Norman hands. De Newburgh then set about the transformation of this Welsh commote into the marcher lordship of Gower. It was essential that the new ruler had a defendable headquarters – or caput – in a convenient place within the lordship. De Newburgh ignored Loughor, which had been the administrative headquarters during Roman times, in favour of the more central and possibly more easily accessible site on the River Tawe.

The motte-and-bailey castle would have been made of wood and would have been built to be as strong as possible. Swansea was at the edge of the Norman possessions in South Wales at this time and the castle could expect to be attacked at any point. Another similar castle was built at Loughor at around the same time, partly on the site of the Roman fort that had existed there. The third castle, this time controlling the upper River Loughor, was at Llandeilo Talybont. Similar motte-and-bailey castles were built at Penmaen and Penrice on Gower.

If King Sweyn Forkbeard had given his name to the spot that the Normans chose for their caput, then Henry de Newburgh would have been aware of it. Only 100 years had passed between Sweyn's death and the arrival of the Normans in south-west Wales. Sweyn was, therefore, a famous figure from the recent past.

Although the Viking age in Britain had ended with the defeat of Harald Hardrada at the Battle of Stamford Bridge in 1066, their activities and exploits were still well remembered. Henry de Newburgh, being a Norman, would have been aware of his descent from those Vikings who settled in France. He may have felt it acceptable to continue using a name that celebrated a fellow Norseman who had also come to the area in search of conquest.

The castle at Swansea served a number of different purposes. It was a military headquarters with a barracks to house soldiers. It was also the centre for the administration of the lordship and was where justice was meted out. Wrongdoers would be held in cells or dungeons, making the castle a prison. There is evidence that coins were minted in Swansea in the twelfth century, so maybe the castle was a mint, too. It certainly would have been the financial headquarters of the lordship and would have included a treasury.

In addition to all of these functions, the castle would also have been home to the lord when he was in the area. It is likely that the de Newburghs would have lived at the castle during the early years of its existence, as the lord would have wanted to keep tight control of developments in his new territory. However, as time went on, and national and international affairs took priority, so the Lords of Gower were content to leave day-to-day control to their steward (also called the seneschal).

The de Newburghs held the Lordship of Gower from 1106 to 1184, when it passed back into the king's hands. He gave it to the de Braose family, who held it until 1326. The de Braoses were renowned as oppressive and cruel in their rule. The last de Braose heiress, Alina, was the daughter of the William de Braose who had died in 1326. She held the castle together with her husband, John de Mowbray.

By the union of Alina with John de Mowbray, the Lordship of Gower passed into the hands of the de Mowbray family. Their son, also called John, repaired the old castle, which had been left badly damaged by the actions of a Welsh princeling, Rhys ap Meredith. (As an aside to these main events in Swansea, it can be noted that John de Mowbray, husband of Alina, was hanged on the battlements at York on the orders of King Edward II.)

Dynastic pressures and marriages meant that by the fifteenth century, the Herberts held the lordship and then it passed to the Somerset family, who were successively Earls and Marquesses of Worcester and Dukes of Beaufort. It remains in that family today.

Imagine, then, a strongly built motte-and-bailey castle on the site of what is today Worcester Place. From the very beginning, there would have been buildings growing up around it. A castle, especially the principal castle of a lordship, would have needed many people to ensure its effective functioning. Being in a hostile country, the most effective way of guaranteeing the loyalty of the people in and around the castle was to bring them in from elsewhere. Swansea would have been populated by immigrant workers, mostly skilled, and their families. Marcher lords could promote the recruiting of immigrant workers without having to obtain permission of the king. With this in mind, the de Newburghs founded the Borough of Swansea, and this was likely to have been before 1158.

The new citizens had to live somewhere, and that had to be as close to the castle as possible. The dwellings clustered around the castle at first, but the closeness of the River Tawe meant that activities like fishing, ship repair and shipbuilding began to develop. Wind Street, which extends in a southerly direction from Castle Bailey Street, would have grown up following the curve of the river, and this can still be seen today. Between it and the river was another road called The Strand. This street is still in existence, and where it joins Oystermouth Road there was, probably in Norman times, a quay.

The lord would have been obliged to provide a church, and the present site of St Mary's Church was the site of the first. It seems that this was rebuilt either five or six times, with the last rebuild taking place after the Second World War, during which it had been destroyed by enemy bombs.

The whole was circled by the town walls, which possibly grew up sometime during the late thirteenth and early fourteenth centuries. It is likely that the little town was protected by a ditch at first, with just a palisade around the castle itself. Once the castle was rebuilt in stone, then continuing the castle walls to form the town's protection would have been quite feasible.

It seems that The Strand lay outside the walls, but they may not have been continuous along this river frontage. The castle would have towered over the riverbank, giving a sense of security to those working and living under its shadow.

Also likely is the existence of four gates into the town. One was situated near St Mary's Church; a second where Wind Street emerged onto the Burrows; a third a little distance

Wesley Chapel, Goat Street.

from the eastern end of Goat Street, which would be today somewhere near the Dragon Hotel, and the fourth on High Street roughly where King's Lane joins High Street today. Both High Street and Wind Street lined up with gates into the castle itself, making it possible for riders to enter both the town and the castle without unnecessary delay.

LIFE IN MEDIEVAL SWANSEA

I have already mentioned the need for the town to be populated by immigrants – people from beyond Wales, to ensure loyalty in the townsfolk. These people would have come from a variety of places, but it would be fair to assume that a significant number of them may well have come from areas in England where the de Newburghs held lands. Some may have come from Normandy, again from places where the de Newburghs held lands. It is also possible that some came from Ireland, especially Dublin.

In order to encourage immigrants to settle in Swansea, inducements would have been offered. These may well have included the promise of a plot to build a house, or the guarantee of a monopoly for a particular trade. Any borough at this time would need a wide range of craftsmen, skilled in particular trades, to make the town a successful and attractive place to live. Included amongst these would be labourers, textile workers, leather workers, carpenters, blacksmiths, boatbuilders, sailors, fishermen, lawyers, scriveners and innkeepers.

There would have been a town mill, run by the miller, and everyone would have been obliged to have their corn ground there. In addition, there would have been bakehouses and brewhouses, so bakers and brewers would have roles to play in the community.

We must not, of course, forget the clerical population, based on St Mary's Church, and the slightly more transient inhabitants of the castle itself. The town was surrounded by its own land, where animals would be kept and agriculture carried out. This probably was organised on the 'strip' system that was common in the medieval period. We know that this system operated at the 'Vile' in Rhosili, so probably was also used on the Swansea lands. The lands that were attached to the town stretched from the Tawe to the Clyne Valley at Blackpill and northwards as far as the Burlais Brook (near Cwmbwrla).

* * *

As we have seen, the town of Swansea was established around 1106 by Henry de Newburgh, who probably gave its burgesses or leading citizens certain rights and privileges. Creating a thriving town required citizens who felt they had a vested interest in its progress, hence the need to give them certain advantages. No charter from the foundation of Swansea survives, if one was ever granted. However, sometime between 1158 and 1184 William de Newburgh, the grandson of the first Lord of Gower, granted a charter to the town. This included the right of burgage tenure, which gave the burgesses of the town freedom from feudal obligations and allowed them to have their own bakehouses and brewhouses, so they weren't required to use those owned by the lord. They were also able to till the fields in the town's land, pasture their livestock there, clear the forest and use wood from the lands to build ships, homes and business premises. They were also granted the right to freely trade through the Port of Swansea, and to fish in the River Tawe.

In 1215, King John granted the town another charter, which was renewed in 1234 and 1322. This charter gave the burgesses of Swansea the right to trade throughout the kingdom and to travel with their merchandise, without having to pay tolls. In 1317 and again in 1338 further charters also allowed the burgesses of the town to charge tolls or customs duties on all commodities sold in the town so that walling and paving could be carried out.

These duties, were known as 'murage' and 'pavage'. They may have paid for repairs to earlier walls, or funded the building of new town walls. I tend to the view that the town walls were already there – it seems unlikely that a town prone to attacks by Welsh dissident forces would have relied just on a ditch for protection. It would have been important for the walls to be kept in good repair. Also, there would have been little point in paving parts of the town's thoroughfares if there was a risk of the buildings being burned to the ground by those forces.

A major charter was agreed in 1306 between the burgesses of Swansea and the overbearing de Braose lord, who was obliged to include provisions to protect the burgesses from the excesses of his governance. They were once again given permission to mine coal and make use of the common land of the town. A particularly important provision, however, was to give the burgesses the right to elect a reeve each year from their own number. The reeve was the equivalent of the mayor in a modern town, but one of his duties was being the contact between the burgesses of the town and the lord, or his representative.

A particularly important privilege that had been granted in an early charter, and then confirmed in subsequent ones, was the right to hold weekly markets and an annual fair. This brought in traders from beyond Swansea, and, of course, an annual fair would be a wonderful and much-anticipated event.

* * *

The growth of the town in the first 200 years of Norman rule was quite rapid, and took Swansea's population to between 1,000 and 1,500 souls. This made it one of the largest Welsh, and indeed European, towns, as the market towns on the Continent tended to be between 500 and 2,000 people. As well as those who lived within the town walls, there were two small communities outside but very close to those walls. The northern gate had a small community just outside it, and the other was on the east side of the river where the ferry crossing had been established.

By 1276 Swansea was a well-established market town and port, probably the most populous in Wales, and was subject therefore to providing support for the plans of King Edward I in his campaign to subdue the remaining independent princes of Wales. Being involved in this way made the town a target for the forces of those princes, and indeed Swansea was attacked by them on more than one occasion.

The town, however, survived and prospered. The port was busy, with ships plying their trade with Bristol, ports on the Bristol Channel, Ireland, the south-west of England and France. Exports would have included leather goods, butter and cheese, timber and wool; exports of coal came later. Imports would have been pottery from France and Bristol, wines from France, cloth, fish and salt. Some luxury goods from further afield would also have come into Swansea by sea.

A shipbuilding industry grew up around the port area, and we know that in the charter of 1306 there was provision for the town to build four 'great ships' every year, plus a number with no limit of smaller craft. These probably were fishing boats, and may well have included those for inshore use.

In 1332, the Bishop of St David's, Henry de Gower, may have been instrumental in the building of an additional section of the castle, referred to as the New Castle, with its distinctive arcading. He also felt that Swansea needed provision for the aged and infirm amongst its population. Accordingly,

A small boat sails into Swansea Harbour, between the East and West Piers. A Newman & Co. print, 1850s.

'Bishop Henry Gower's Palace, being an addition to Swansea Castle in the fourteenth century', published by Godfrey, 1786.

he founded and endowed the Hospital of the Blessed David to provide accommodation for them. Almshouses like this were being provided all over the kingdom, so such a foundation was not unique to Swansea. Part of the original building still survives as part of the Cross Keys public house opposite St Mary's Church. It is not known whether the Lady Alina, who resided at the Old Castle at this time, was involved in the funding of the hospital. She may well have been a patroness of the bishop, and would doubtless have been charitable towards his foundation.

The role played by Bishop Henry in the building of the New Castle has been subject to a great deal of speculation, based on the fact that the distinctive arcading can also be found on the Bishop's Palace at St David's and also on the one at Lamphey. Was he so impressed by this architectural feature that he had it incorporated into his Swansea residence? It is also possible that Lord John de Mowbray or his steward, when deciding to build the additional accommodation at the castle, employed the architect who had designed the palaces for the bishop.

TOIL AND TROUBLE

The twelfth to the fourteenth centuries had been a golden period, both for Swansea and indeed the kingdom as a whole. Historically, there was a sense of settled prosperity, certainly in England, and although there were always problems in France and parts of Wales, the ordinary folk were mostly able to carry on with their domestic lives. Towns grew as trade blossomed, production of food was stable and monasteries were able to promote learning and build dramatic monastic churches.

However, this was about to come to an end as the continent of Europe entered a period of social upheaval and economic turmoil. Firstly came famine between 1315 and 1317. Crops failed and food shortages were such that thousands of people died. Swansea may not have suffered as badly as other parts of Europe, although the effects of famine would have been felt in the town as corn, especially, which had been imported from France and other areas of Europe, would no longer be available.

This was followed by the Black Death of 1349–51 and subsequent outbreaks of plague through the next 200 years. Ports and coastal communities suffered badly when plague broke out, so it is likely that Swansea also suffered the effects of these recurrent outbreaks. The population would have been decimated during severe outbreaks and this is supported by the fact that, by Tudor times, fewer than 900 people lived in the town.

Other factors that added to the problems for many towns, including Swansea, were the demands by the Kings of England between 1337 and 1453 (the period of the Hundred Years War) for more financial support from the whole country. This led to greater taxation, which in turn led to higher inflation and currency depreciation. In Wales, this was added to the problems arising from the activities of Owain Glyndwr between 1400 and 1410.

The combined effects of war, plague and rebellion would have affected most towns, and in Swansea there is evidence to show that the revenues accruing to the lord were in decline. Rents, tolls and court revenues dropped by 80 per cent in some instances. On top of that, there were examples of fraud on the part of certain officials, and the awareness of the burgesses that opportunities were arising where they could demand further safeguards and privileges from the Lord of Gower.

However, Swansea started to recover from the problems that had beset it over the previous couple of centuries. Change was on the way, and these came as a result of a change of monarch. The Welsh-born Henry Tudor defeated King Richard III at Bosworth Field and took the throne as King Henry VII. The Tudor age, an era of momentous developments, had dawned.

TUDOR SWANSEA

King Henry VIII was instrumental in the passing of legislation, the Act of Union, which completely restructured the local government of Wales. Passed between 1536 and 1543, the legislation removed the marcher lordships as the basis for administration in Wales and replaced them with a system that copied the English shire approach. The Lordship of

Gower was attached to Glamorgan, which became a shire county. Swansea lost its status as a caput of a lordship, although it retained its status as a borough. Cardiff became the county town and therefore the administrative centre of the new Glamorganshire. Further west, its natural former bedfellows became the county of Carmarthenshire, with Carmarthen as the county town. Swansea was now forced to look east, rather than west. So, downgraded and humiliated, Swansea would seem to be destined for the decline that most other former caputs suffered.

However, this was not the case at all. Swansea had some natural advantages, which were denied to other former caputs. It had size, to begin with, having previously been the largest town in Wales. Even with the decline in population caused by the plagues that it had suffered, it was still a large town by contemporary Welsh standards. It was a port, and a busy and popular one, too.

As a market town, Swansea continued to attract people from the surrounding countryside on market days. There were now two markets held every week, one on Wednesday and one on Saturday. In addition to this, Swansea now had three fairs annually. These attracted traders from much further afield, who came to buy and sell livestock. Fairs also brought itinerant entertainers, who served to delight and divert the inhabitants. The town now boasted an increased range of skilled craftsmen, as specialisation in particular areas of production intensified. Glovers, hatters, tilers, vintners, shoemakers, masons and pavers all joined the list of trades in the town.

A direct result of the Act of Union was that Wales was now able to return Members of Parliament. Swansea became one of the boroughs that had a say in the return of a Member of Parliament for the Glamorgan boroughs. It was the burgesses of the town who had an important role to play in this

A rumbustious scene at the Cromwellian market in Swansea, drawn by John Nixon in 1799.

election. The burgesses were the leading citizens of the town, and from their number the Council of the Borough was selected. The members of the council were aldermen, an elite within an elite. The council annually nominated two of their number to be considered for portreeve (the title had grown since medieval times, and was now the equivalent of mayor). The lord or his steward then chose which of the two would be portreeve for the upcoming year.

To be a burgess, one had to inherit the position, marry the daughter of a burgess, be an apprentice to a burgess or receive it by gift of the corporation. In effect, this limited the number of burgesses, and whilst there was no maximum number of burgesses laid down, it was in their own interests to keep the number low. There were considerable perks to being a burgess, and as several of these were financial, having too large a number would affect the finances of the corporation.

Burgesses did not pay tolls on merchandise that came into the town, nor did they pay to undertake trade within the town. Another perk was communal trading, where goods coming into the town had to be offered to the burgesses before any could be sold to the ordinary folk. The burgesses' needs came before those of anyone else. In addition to these commercial advantages, the corporation also held feasts twice a year, at Easter and Michaelmas, and on other occasions where rejoicing seemed appropriate.

The lord himself had good reason to keep the numbers of burgesses as low as possible. Now that burgesses had a say in the election of a Member of Parliament, the lord would wish to maintain some influence and control over the electoral process. There were no secret ballots at this time, so how the votes were cast was common knowledge. The lord would have a favoured candidate, and would wish to know how his burgesses were voting. Perhaps pressure could be brought to bear on those likely to defy the lord's wishes.

Mostly, the corporation was concerned with the corporation's finances, controlling trade within the town and provision for the poor. Another body that had some control over aspects of the life of the town was the parish. This body was led by the portreeve, and had responsibility for the upkeep of the highways and bridges, the provision and supervision of the jail and exterminating vermin, as well as provision for the poor, and disabled soldiers and sailors come upon hard times. Providing relief for the poor was partly covered by the Hospital of Blessed David.

At this point, there needs to be some explanation regarding the area covered by Swansea parish. The River Tawe was the boundary between the Lordship of Gower and the Lordship of Kilvey. Both were held by the same lord but were administered separately. The Lordship of Kilvey was very much smaller than that of Gower. It comprised 10¾ square miles, whereas the Lordship of Gower encompassed some 157 square miles.

Of the Lordship of Kilvey, the bulk was within the parish of Llansamlet, and a small part, at the southern edge adjoining the sea, was the hamlet of St Thomas, which was part of the parish of Swansea. The name of the hamlet came from the Chapel of St Thomas the Martyr, which stood at the edge of the sea. This little chapel does have one claim to a place in the history books, as it was here in 1321 that the Welshmen of Kilvey forced Edward II's escheator to turn back when he tried to occupy Gower in the king's name. Subsequently, they were forced to yield to Guy Almavini, the king's sergeant, and his men. This was the trigger for the Barons' Revolt, which led to the murder of King Edward at Berkeley Castle in Gloucestershire. Gower was then restored to John de Mowbray, son of Alina, and so she avenged the execution of her husband at York by the king.

From time to time, the burgesses would try to assert some independence from the lord, but it was in the general interest of the town to have the lord onside, especially when he had influence at Court and in the government. Tudor governments, unlike earlier ones, did endeavour to encourage trade and help the country to prosper. The Act of Union itself brought Wales into the English system, and so government policy would apply there as well. Trade was of paramount concern, and its encouragement was one of the bedrocks of Tudor policy. Having already made changes to the local government system in Wales, efforts to streamline other areas of commercial life were made.

Attempts were made at the beginning of the reign of Queen Elizabeth to bring some order to the customs regime along the coast of Wales. Swansea, at first, was subordinate to Cardiff, which had acquired the status of Head Port. This must have been deemed inappropriate, as in 1573 Swansea was given its own customs house. Like many new systems, this customs reorganisation took some time to settle, with all sorts of accusations being made about bribery and the accepting of favours. Doubtless illegal exporting and importing went on, but whether this was as a result of corruption, we cannot say.

However, the biggest upheaval in the life of the whole of both England and Wales came about as a result of the Reformation. Henry VIII imposed Protestantism on the population of the country for purely personal and dynastic reasons. However, this was not an alien religion being imposed arbitrarily. Protestantism was just a branch of the Christian faith which chose to follow different practices to those of the Catholic Church. There were many Protestant sympathisers in both England and Wales before the Reformation, and Henry was aware that his religious revolution would be welcomed in some quarters, and probably not opposed by much of the ordinary population.

The practices of the Catholic Church were swept away, along with the Pope's authority. Royal supremacy took its place, and a Protestant prayer book was introduced, with simpler church services taking place in unadorned churches. The monasteries and monastic orders ceased to function, and indeed many were to benefit from the redistribution of monastic lands and buildings.

In Swansea, there doesn't seem to have been much objection to the changes, although doubtless there were heated arguments between citizens. However, none of these boiled over into riot or damage. Indeed it has been suggested that Swansea people did harbour some Puritan sympathies, which were to become more noticeable in the next century.

Sketch of the 1585 town hall, drawn around 1780.

Up until the reign of King James I, the corporation of Swansea met in a building called the Shyre House, on or very near Castle Bailey Street where Plas House later stood. In the next reign, that of King Charles I, the corporation decided that they needed to have a meeting place of their own and, accordingly, a new town hall was built at the eastern edge of the bailey yard of the castle and fronted Castle Bailey Street, but on the opposite side. This comprised two floors with the Upper Hall being used for meetings, and the Lower Hall, on the ground floor, serving as a store for burgesses 'privileged goods' and supplies for the poor.

It must also be noted that, by the time of the Tudors, Swansea had developed an embryonic industry that was going to lead to it becoming a frontrunner in the Industrial Revolution. This was coal mining, which had been carried on in the area for generations. First mentioned in 1306, it had obviously been undertaken for years prior to that date. By the time of Elizabeth I, there was a flourishing, if small-scale, export industry. This coal was used for domestic heating and cooking and had a reputation as a quality fuel.

THE CIVIL WAR AND COMMONWEALTH

When the conflict between Parliament and King Charles I erupted into open warfare, Swansea seemed to be ready to give its support to the king. The Earl of Worcester, who was Lord of Gower, wholeheartedly supported the king. He was both wealthy and influential, and therefore a valued ally of the monarch. In the town, the local gentry and leading merchants also declared for the king. However, the earlier Puritan sympathies were also influencing some of the minor gentry and ordinary citizens. One such was a certain Philip Jones of Llangyfelach. He was a Puritan who left Swansea to fight in the Parliamentary armies, rising to the rank of colonel.

Swansea was a base of considerable importance to the Royalist cause. It was a garrison town, site of a royal arsenal, and a port through which supplies could be shipped. However, in 1645 it fell to the Parliamentary forces. Colonel Philip Jones was made governor.

In 1648 Oliver Cromwell visited Swansea, possibly to inspect his new acquisition, for he had been made Lord of Gower the year before. He instructed the corporation to construct a new 'market house' in Castle Square, which would replace the rather haphazard arrangements for the earlier market along Wind Street and under the walls of the castle.

The new building opened in 1651 and remained the main market building in Swansea until 1822. The market house roof was made of lead, which had evidently been stolen by Colonel Philip Jones from the roof of St David's Cathedral during the time that Cromwell was in Pembrokeshire, accompanied by the colonel. For many years, this story was considered to be just that, a story, but later documents show that it was probably true.

Philip Jones was an able soldier and leader, but tended towards unscrupulous actions when he thought he could get away with it. He rose to be the Comptroller of Oliver Cromwell's household, and he thus became one of the most powerful figures in Britain and, for a few years at least, became the most influential man in Glamorganshire. At the end of the conflict, when the Restoration was about to begin, he managed to save for his family the castle and estate of Fonmon in south Glamorgan, where he was then living.

The effect of the Civil War on Swansea was extremely damaging. Having been a Royalist town that was then attacked and taken for the Parliamentarians, there would have been damage, both physical and to the town's trade. Efforts were made during the settled period of the Commonwealth to stimulate trade and bring the port back to full use. The war had seen the markets closed, fairs abandoned and the municipal income of the town drop. These had to be addressed and, to some extent, the town's prosperity was eventually to improve.

Through the years of the Commonwealth, Swansea saw much change in the religious nature of the town. Puritanism had already taken hold, with a small Puritan church being founded in 1642. After 1645, with the Royalist cause defeated, a number of Nonconformist churches were established. Independents, Baptists, Quakers and Presbyterians all had ministers active in the town and growing congregations to which to minister.

In 1650, the government passed the Propagation Act, which enabled the provision of schools in Wales. This was the first time that the state had become involved with the provision of schools and had taken any responsibility for the education of the population. One school was established in Swansea but it seems it was not particularly successful.

THE RESTORATION PERIOD IN SWANSEA

Although the later years of the Commonwealth were mostly peaceful, and some return to normal trading conditions was possible, recovery was slow, and it was only after the Restoration that a long period of stability was ensured. The people of Swansea were jubilant in their celebration of King Charles II's return to the throne. This suggested that they had not been wholly in favour of the restrictions on ordinary life that the Parliamentarians had implemented. It seems 1660, therefore, was a year to be remembered.

With the monarchy restored, the ruling classes were once again established in their traditional roles, and the Anglican Church returned to its former role. In a town that was growing, it was inevitable that a proportion of the population would be Dissenters, that is, those who rejected the authority of the Anglican Church. There was a feeling among some prominent Anglicans that they needed to fight fire with fire to prevent the wider spread of this religious dissent, and adopt some of the tactics that the Puritans had used during the Commonwealth.

Bishop Hugh Gore opened a grammar school to encourage 'virtue and good literature' in the boys of the town. The aim would have been to give the boys a sound training in academic subjects, instil discipline and give them a moral basis for their lives. Such an education would have brought them opportunities for a future in trade and the professions and indeed, for some, maybe a career in the Church. Although the Anglican Church was keen to limit the spread of the Dissenters, it was not unknown for them to work in tandem to oppose immorality and ignorance in the population. Swansea had its fair share of both.

This would have been an increasingly onerous undertaking, as the population was growing, along with the rest of Wales. In 1670, hearth tax returns suggest a population of between 1,400 and 1,600. This, of course, does not take into account those who had, for various reasons, managed to evade the tax. By adding in an estimated figure for those, we can suggest a figure of maybe 1,750 people. By the turn of the eighteenth century, estimates based on births and deaths put the population at about 1,830, but there was a sizeable Dissenting population whose records would not appear in the Anglican registers. Including these would take the population up to perhaps 2,500. The activities of Dissenting ministers like Stephen Hughes, the nicknamed 'Apostle of Carmarthenshire' who was resident in Swansea, encouraged Dissenters to settle in the town. This was technically illegal, but there doesn't seem to have been any concerted attempt to prevent this settlement.

The population of Swansea was rising because the town was becoming more prosperous. The port was one of the busiest, the embryonic coal industry was becoming established and there was a strong agricultural economy in the areas around the town. Exports of live animals such as sheep, pigs and cattle were growing. The production and export of butter, cheese and cereal grains was also increasing. This was helped by the years of relative peace that followed the Restoration. The travails of the Stuart kings after the death of Charles II, and the consequent Glorious Revolution which brought William III and Mary II jointly to the throne, had few repercussions for the lives of ordinary folk.

The changes that were about to happen were not the result of politically inspired events but were triggered by visionary men who saw economic advantage in industry. Swansea's future was about to alter dramatically. The industrial age was about to ensure those changes.

3

SWANSEA'S ALTER EGO

THE TOWN IN THE LATE EIGHTEENTH AND EARLY NINETEENTH CENTURIES

From about 1760 through to the end of the Regency period, Swansea was able to show the world a genteel face, where pursuit of the arts, literature and science could be undertaken in conducive circumstances by both the local gentry and visitors to the town.

HOUSES FOR THE GENTRY

One of the most noticeable features of Swansea, both then and today, is the preponderance of houses belonging to the gentry that exist in the area between Brynmill and Clyne. Sketty seemed to be a particular magnet for well-to-do families who had made their money as industrialists. These houses include an octagonal villa built in 1773 for Edward King, the Comptroller of Customs for the Port of Swansea. John Henry Vivian later bought this building and incorporated it into his new residence, Singleton Abbey. Nearby was an earlier house named Verandah, which had been built by a Captain Rawleigh Mansel. He died whilst serving in the West Indies, and his widow married the second Richard Calvert Jones. John

Henry Vivian bought the house in about 1840, as it was so close to his new abbey.

On the road from Sketty to Swansea there stood a farm that had a long history. Called 'Parc Wern', it was bought by Captain Frederick Hickey RN, who built a substantial house in which he was resident from about 1817. In 1840, John Henry Vivian bought it, intending to put it to use as a dower house – that is, a home for his wife Sarah after he had died. Things did not work out quite as intended though, for in 1855 on John Henry's death, she refused to move out of Singleton, and his heir, Hussey remained at Parc Wern. Hussey's sister Dulcie inherited the house, and during the Great War she allowed it to be used as a hospital. Now known as Parc Beck it has become student accommodation.

Sketty Hall, a mansion dating from the 1720s when it was called New Hall, was, at different times, home to a number of well-known gentlemen in the Swansea elite. Built by Rawleigh Dawkin, it passed to Mansel Dawkin, his brother. It was then bought by Charles Baring, the London merchant banker. Other residents included Ralph Sheldon MP; Richard Mansel Phillips, who was Mayor of Swansea from 1836–37; Lewis Weston Dillwyn MP; William Jenkins, the ship owner; Frank Ash Yeo MP; and Richard Glynn Vivian, Hussey Vivian's youngest brother. It was Richard Glynn Vivian who gave Swansea the art gallery which still bears his name. Ultimately, Swansea Corporation bought the house and land and built Bishop Gore School in one corner of the estate. Sketty Hall was used as a research centre by the British Steel Corporation for a time and today is part of Gower College Swansea.

John Morris, whose copperworks dominated the Lower Swansea Valley at this time, built a mansion in the Palladian style called 'Clasemont'. Unfortunately, it was a house that, due to its position, suffered rather badly from the smoke, fumes and acrid smells that hung over the Lower Swansea Valley at this time. Morris therefore demolished Clasemont and build a new house in Sketty called Sketty Park House. It is said that most of the resultant debris from the demolition was brought from Clasemont – a feat achieved in one night – and used in the building of the new house. It remained in the Morris family until 1930, when the Swansea Corporation bought it. After several disparate uses, it was demolished in 1975 and the whole of the parkland became the Sketty Park housing estate.

Another house, called 'Hafod', had been built by the Morris family in a corner of Sketty Park. This was demolished in around 1900. Its site is now occupied by Parklands School, while in the north-western corner of the old Sketty Park stands another school, Olchfa.

Other large houses in this area that were occupied by members of the gentry include 'Sketty Isha' and 'Derwen Fawr', both of which became part of the Bible College in the 1930s.

Today, Clyne Gardens in Blackpill are a deserved feather in the cap of Swansea City Council Parks Department. The house and gardens at Clyne came into the corporation's ownership in 1952 on the death of Admiral Algernon Walker Heneage-Vivian. Clyne Castle, as the house is known, was transferred to Swansea University but the gardens, with their magnificent collections of rhododendrons, became a public park.

Swansea's Parks Department has a reputation beyond the boundaries of Swansea for the quality and upkeep of the many parks and gardens in the city. The efforts in the Regency period to create walks and gardens for the pleasure of both visitors and residents of the town certainly influenced later developments. By the 1870s, the work done by William Thomas of Lan in creating an 'Open Spaces Movement' in Swansea, encouraged others.

John Dillwyn Llewellyn gifted a farm called 'Cnap Llwyd' to the town for the creation of a park, and subsequently it became Parc Llewellyn. William Thomas himself managed to save a considerable amount of land around St Helen's from development. This opened in 1887 and, to mark the Queen's Golden Jubilee, it was named Victoria Park. The present Victoria Park is much reduced, as in 1934 the new Guildhall was built at the eastern edge. Also, Dame Adelina Patti's gift of the Winter Gardens from Craig-y-Nos Castle was erected in the park, as the Patti Pavilion, in 1920.

Altogether, Swansea now boasts fifty-two parks and gardens.

Woodland Castle, which was later renamed Clyne Castle. This view dates from 1824.

SEASIDE RESORT AND SPA TOWN

Before the dominance of the town by the industrial development of the nineteenth century, Swansea had a reputation as a seaside resort and spa town. Visitors in the late eighteenth century were able to spend time in a town that came to rival Bath as a destination for the fashionistas of the Regency period. The visitor could attend soirees in the Assembly Rooms, take the sea air on a carriage drive along the beach, participate in the cure by sea bathing or take health-giving walks along the river.

One of the innovative attractions on the Burrows was the Bathing House, provided for the convenience of those wishing to ready themselves for a dip in the sea. This building, however, seems to have been no longer in use for its original purpose when, in 1817, it was taken over by the Board of Guardians and became the Swansea Workhouse in one part, the other part becoming the Swansea Infirmary.

The fashionable area of Swansea, around the Burrows, largely developed around the period from 1800 to about 1830. As the name implies, this area was one of sand dunes, and much of it was developed to the designs of the Swansea architect, William Jernegan. He also designed the Assembly Rooms, which were opened in 1821, and the Countess of Huntingdon's Chapel.

Outdoor entertainment was considered just as important, and in 1785 the Duke of Beaufort was responsible for the creation of a public walk on the Burrows. From 1789, corporation-owned pleasure gardens existed on the Burrows, and these continued to be maintained by the corporation until the building of the South Dock in the 1850s. The area around the Burrows was important as a fashionable recreational area, and the corporation would only grant permission for the building of houses that met with certain criteria. From

1810, a project providing walks and gardens was instigated by Sir John Morris and in 1816, in order to maintain the exclusivity of these features, gates and walls were erected.

The fashionable elite who came to Swansea, either to stay at one of the better hotels in town or with friends at one of the residences in the Sketty area, would need to be entertained. With this in mind, the first theatre to open – the Swansea Theatre, just off Wind Street – opened its doors in 1780. It proved to be an immediate success, and it was decided that the town could accommodate a larger one. Consequently, the Theatre Royal was opened in 1807 on the corner of Bank Street and Goat Street, which today is the corner of Castle Gardens and Princess Way, where the clothes retailers Zara have their shop.

Sports of various kinds began to take root during the early years of the nineteenth century. One of the most spectacular, with crowds of fashionable supporters, was horse racing. These early organised races took place on Crymlyn Burrows, on the east side of the river. This necessitated punters to cross the river by ferry or ford. Another sporting tradition that developed from around this time was the regatta, with both sailing and rowing competitions. Even today Swansea boasts two yacht clubs.

One sport that had been played in an unorganised and rather haphazard way by ordinary folk was cricket – another was football. Cricket made the leap across the social divide first, during the 1770s and 1780s. There were probably cricket games on Crymlyn Burrows in these first years, but it was to find a permanent home further along Swansea Bay, on a field on the St Helen's Estate of Colonel Llewellyn Morgan. Once established there, it stayed, and the St Helen's Cricket Ground still exists.

Other sports were to become established, as with various popular forms of entertainment, but that came after the end of the Regency period. Homegrown entertainment involving the sons of the gentry had, of necessity, grown up between the 1780s and the 1830s. Europe was in turmoil across those years, with the French Revolution, the Revolutionary and Napoleonic Wars and with continuing revolutionary fervour lingering after peace had broken out. This had meant no grand tours for the posh boys; no travelling to Mediterranean climes, seeing the sights in Rome or Athens. There was less chance to meet a wealthy heiress – although they would have had to have been Italian or Austrian, or whatever. The wealthy British heiresses tended to travel less, and stay in good old Blighty. There would be no gathering of romantic experiences either. This is why British seaside towns and spas did so well in those years, as the gentry had to look closer to home for their fun. After about 1830, though, Europe was open for business once more and the British resorts began to decline. In Swansea, however, the heyday being over mattered much less, because industry could now be the creator of wealth.

THE CAMBRIAN AND GLAMORGAN POTTERIES

The Cambrian Pottery was founded in 1764 by William Coles on a site close to today's High Street Station. At first, it used locally sourced clay to produce rough pottery products intended for the local market. It was common for potteries of this kind to manufacture items that were considered almost disposable – they were cheap to replace should they be broken. However, by the 1780s the Cambrian had progressed to using a better-quality clay imported from Devon and Dorset to produce a range of finer-quality earthenware pottery.

In 1789, Coles' son John entered into a partnership with a Quaker from Warwickshire named George Haynes. Seeing the potential that the pottery had, Haynes undertook the reorganisation of the business based on the principles used by Josiah Wedgwood in Staffordshire. He even brought a number of skilled pottery workers from Staffordshire down to Swansea. Swansea Corporation was in a much more obliging mood at this time – with the obstructionist Gabriel Powell now dead, there was a new willingness to promote the development of industry in the town – and they granted Haynes new leases. In just a year, four new kilns were up and running and there were new buildings on the site.

The pottery was now able to supply the growing local demand for high-quality porcelain products. As the town became wealthier, so the families of those newly successful industrialists and entrepreneurs wanted dinner sets, tea services, special plates for dessert and for supper, in a variety of shapes, sizes and designs and, of course, of the best possible quality.

Indeed, the quality of the wares produced by the Cambrian Pottery was high, and attracted a market beyond Swansea. At first sales grew in the West Country, but this was soon followed by increasing exports to eastern Europe, the Mediterranean countries and as far as the West Indies and the USA. The pottery also produced vases and ornaments for display on mantelpieces and, in an age when painting was a desirable pursuit for young ladies of good birth, bisque porcelain for them to paint at their leisure.

In 1802, Lewis Weston Dillwyn became a partner and in 1810 Haynes left the company, having fallen out with Dillwyn. The following year, Dillwyn took T. & J. Bevington into partnership, and over the next few years, the famed Swansea Porcelain reached its peak of quality and desirability. In the meantime, Haynes opened the Glamorgan Pottery next door to the Cambrian, launching a range of products that were essentially intended for domestic use. It seems there was sufficient demand for quality pottery to enable a second business to also be successful.

Back at the Cambrian Pottery, Lewis Llewellyn Dillwyn, son of Lewis Weston Dillwyn, took over the running of the pottery in 1836. When, in 1838, the Glamorgan Pottery was put up for sale, Dillwyn bought it, closed it and sold the assets to William Chambers, who then opened the South Wales Pottery in Llanelly, launching in 1840.

BANKING

Discussion of the events surrounding the opening of another pottery in Swansea brings us on to the financing of that venture. Whilst the corporation was much more willing to assist in the granting of leases for land to be developed, the capital had to come from somewhere. For Haynes, he was in a good position to access funds, as he owned a bank.

Traditionally, banking up to the time of the Reformation and the dissolution of the monasteries had been in the hands of the Church, or the moneylenders that existed in every town. By the eighteenth century, though, the increasingly complex financial arrangements that were needed to fund the Industrial Revolution necessitated a new approach.

The Bank of England came into existence in 1694, and would have an important role to play later in the story of banking in Swansea. Private banks began to proliferate, reflecting the pace of industrial development from the late 1700s into the nineteenth century. The first banks in

Glamorganshire opened in Merthyr Tydfil, the county's largest town, in the early 1770s.

Haynes, however, was not the first to open a bank in Swansea. That honour goes to Herbert Mackworth, who opened such facilities in Neath and Swansea in the early 1780s. This Swansea bank was taken over by Thomas Maddocks, one of Swansea's aldermen, in 1791, with another, the Swansea Bank, owned by two prominent tradesmen, Walters and Voss, opening at the same time. Haynes' bank did not open until 1800, with offices in High Street.

In the next century more banks opened. The Swansea & Llanelly Union Bank opened in 1810. This was a partnership between Thomas Mansfield and Henry Child, who were evidently attracted to Swansea by the entrepreneurial opportunities they recognised in the town. The already established Swansea, Neath & Glamorganshire Bank was taken over by two Quakers, Robert Eaton and Joseph Gibbins, who came to the town in 1811 and took over the business.

After a couple of decades of growth in the banking sphere, not just in Swansea but nationwide, a spanner was thrown into the works when the country was hit by a financial crisis in 1825. The Haynes Bank and that of Gibbins & Eaton, amongst others, were forced to suspend payments. A period of financial turmoil followed into 1826.

New legislation was introduced, allowing the establishment of branch banks and the Bank of England itself began to consider suitable locations for its own branches. The movers and shakers in Swansea did not see any reason why one of those branches should not be in their town. They acted quickly, sent a delegation to the Bank of England in London, and pressed the case for a branch in Swansea. Ultimately, they were successful and, against competition from Cardiff, Newport and Merthyr Tydfil,

Swansea was chosen to host a branch, which opened on 23 October 1826 – only the third Bank of England branch in Britain. Swansea, as a result, was now the main financial centre for South Wales. Confidence returned in the financial sector and several new banks were opened.

4

INDUSTRIAL DEVELOPMENT AND THE LOWER SWANSEA VALLEY

INDUSTRIAL SWANSEA

The growth of industrial Swansea can be traced in no small part to the arrival in the town in 1716 of Dr John Lane. Dr Lane was a distinguished surgeon and physician. However, he also was experimenting with metallurgical processes. In 1694, he became a partner with Thomas Collins and his father-in-law John Pollard, in a copper-smelting works in Neath Abbey. For some reason, this did not work out favourably and the partnership was dissolved in 1716, with Dr Lane moving to Swansea.

He was looking for a suitable site for his own copper-works, as he had developed a process for smelting copper that required access to a ready supply of cheap coal. Coal had been mined in the area since the early Middle Ages, and by the beginning of the eighteenth century a body of expertise had been built up along with a thriving export trade.

The coal that came through Swansea's port was mostly used for domestic fuel, but that was about to change. The needs of the copper-smelting industry – and there were fourteen more copperworks opened during the height of

Blast furnaces, Lower Swansea Valley, 1881.

the Industrial Revolution, mostly in the Lower Swansea Valley – meant that the local market needed more coal, and pits were dug through the area to supply that demand. As with coal mining, a body of expertise built up so that other metallurgical industries grew up in the area. Lead and zinc were prominent, and a century or so later, tinplate.

COPPER

Copper smelting had been tried at other locations, but without much success, and consequently smelted copper had to be imported. From 1680, however, when copper ore was discovered in Cornwall and a new process for smelting that ore was devised, it became obvious that it was cheaper to take the ore to the coal than vice versa. Three tons of coal was needed to smelt 1 ton of copper ore, so the costs of carrying the ore would have been less than for the coal.

Fortunately, the nearest supply of suitable coal was at the western end of the South Wales coalfield, around Swansea. Swansea also had a suitable harbour for the import of the ore and a river that was navigable for about 3 miles inland. The establishment of the smelting works along the River Tawe meant that the ships carrying the ore could sail far enough upriver to unload at quays alongside the works. Flat land on either side of the river at this point meant that works could be built easily.

In addition to this, coal was in demand in Cornwall to fuel the pumping engines that were used to pump water out of the mines. Being bereft of coal, the Cornish mine owners had to seek it elsewhere and, by chance, the area around Swansea had much coal. The ships carrying the copper ore could therefore return with cargoes of coal, much to the profit of the shipowners.

Dr Lane seems to have been in partnership once again with John Pollard, and they opened the Llangyfelach Works in 1717. Lane was not, it appeared, a wise businessman, investing heavily in the South Sea Company. When this failed – an event known to history as the 'South Sea Bubble' – he was bankrupted. He returned to Bristol, and resumed practising medicine. Control of his business then passed to his supervising manager, Robert Morris, in 1824.

Morris had come from Shropshire to take up this post, and it proved to be a sensible move on his part. Two years later, he was in control of the company, setting up a partnership called Lockwood, Morris & Company. The Morris family were to be entrenched as one of the main industrialists for more than

100 years. The township of Morriston is named after Robert's son, John Morris, who built it as a place for his workers to live. The Morris' copperworks moved from Landore in 1748 and then, in 1793, they built new works back at Landore.

Over the next forty or so years, other industrialists opened copperworks in the Lower Swansea Valley. Entrepreneurs were encouraged by what they had seen already and followed in Dr Lane's footsteps. Thomas Coster & Company opened at White Rock in 1737 and Chauncey Townsend opened at Middle Bank in 1755 and Upper Bank in 1757.

None of these were local men. Chauncey Townsend came from London, and the Costers were from Bristol. The Vivians were of Cornish stock who also had interests in several Cornish mines. Other copperworks were opened by companies with copper ore mining interests in Anglesey, which was itself developing as a source of ore. The Parys Mine Company came to Upper Bank in 1782 and the Stanley Company opened at Middle Bank in 1787 and then another at Penclawdd.

Llangyfelach Copperworks, Landore, Swansea, around 1750.

Some manufacturers of copper products, irked by the monopolistic practices of the existing smelters, opened their own smelting works in the area. The Birmingham Mining & Copper Company was one, arriving in 1793. Four years later, the Rose Copper Company also opened its own smelter.

By 1800, altogether some seven copperworks existed in the area, with a further one out at Penclawdd. This had similar advantages, being on the coast and near a supply of coal. This works had been founded in 1800 by John Vivian, as a partner in the Cheadle Brassware Company. In 1809, however, he split from that company and built his own copperworks at the Hafod. The Vivian family came to dominate the copper industry in the town and became leading citizens.

One of the last companies to open a copperworks in Swansea was Williams, Foster & Company. Their Morfa Works was opened adjacent to the Hafod Works and was destined to become the largest of all the Swansea copper-smelting works. Michael Williams of this company was also a Cornishman, as were the Grenfell family, who came to own works at Middle Bank and Upper Bank in the nineteenth century.

Before the 1820s, the output of copper ore from the Parys Mountain on Anglesey was beginning to decline. This coincided with an increase in the demand for copper and, although the Cornish mines were still producing, it became necessary to seek ore from elsewhere. The gap was filled with ore from South America, especially Chile and Cuba. Later, ore also came into Swansea from Spain, South Africa, Canada and Australia.

The sourcing of ore from these more distant countries was ultimately to affect the industry in Swansea and led to its decline. These countries began to supply a partially smelted ore known as regulus. This saved on transport costs but the ability to produce regulus meant that a first step had been taken in the smelting process and, logically, it made sense for a full smelting industry to be developed in situ. The finished copper ingots could then be exported, making transport costs very much lower indeed. Ore continued to come into the town from Cornwall up until about 1870, and from other sources thereafter.

Swansea's given nickname, 'Copperopolis', had been well earned, and the copper ore barques that brought the ore from South America, usually around Cape Horn, presented a rather romantic image as they sailed in the town's harbour. By the turn of the twentieth century, however, it was clear that Swansea had lost its pre-eminence. Copperworks closures took place throughout the twentieth century, with the combined Hafod-Morfa copperworks closing in 1980, the largest and last of Swansea's great copper smelting houses.

One of the famous copper ore barques being towed into harbour in 1839, by John Weir Padley.

ZINC

The industry in the Lower Swansea Valley and its environs was not limited to just copper, however. In 1883, when activity in the valley was at its height, there were 124 works of various kinds, yet only twelve of those were copper-works. The availability of skilled workers in the smelting of metal brought other practitioners to the area. Zinc and lead, which had been smelted by Chauncey Townsend in 1755 at his Middle Bank Works, were two important metals. Townsend went on to smelt both at his Upper Bank Works from 1757. However, later owners of those works abandoned them and went over to smelting copper. It was not until 1832, when G.F. Muntz perfected his alloy of copper and zinc, that zinc smelting took off in the area. Muntz produced this yellow metal alloy himself at Upper Bank, although it was later manufactured under licence by the Vivians. The alloy became popular as it could be used to sheath the hulls of ships for far less cost than using the much more expensive copper sheeting.

The second innovation to involve zinc was the creation, in 1837, of galvanised iron – corrugated iron – which immediately found favour as a cheap building and roofing material. In dry countries such as those in Southern Africa, South America and Australia, it became a ubiquitous building material. The demand for zinc subsequently soared, and as a result the Vivians converted their old Birmingham copperworks to zinc smelting, and Pascoe Grenfell added zinc smelting to their copperworks at Upper Bank. A new works, the Cambrian Smelting Works, had been set up in 1836 and was later taken over by L. Llewellyn Dillwyn. This works remained open until 1926.

More zinc smelters opened over the next half-century. These were the Crown Works, which became the English

Crown Works at Port Tennant in 1866. Jennings & Co. set up in the same year, and then the Villiers Spelter Company in 1873. The Swansea Vale Company was founded in 1876, with the Swansea Zinc Ore Company coming along ten years later.

These works all changed hands often over the next forty years, and all but one had closed by 1930. The Swansea Vale Works became part of the Imperial Smelting Corporation and survived until 1971.

LEAD

Lead was smelted in the eighteenth century by both Dr Lane and Chauncey Townsend, but the enterprise was unsuccessful and they turned their whole attention to copper smelting, as we have seen. In 1870 the White Rock Works were acquired as a joint venture between Vivian & Sons and Williams Foster. They adapted the works for the smelting of lead and silver and carried on this business for some fifty years, by which time it had become the sole property of the Vivians. Lead smelting peaked towards the end of the nineteenth century, but by 1910 the industry seemed to be in terminal decline, although there was brief respite during the First World War, when production was boosted by the demands of the War Office. Lead smelting at White Rock finally stopped in 1923.

TINPLATE

The process of tinning thin sheets of iron was not new in the eighteenth century. The process had been understood for several hundred years and had probably first been discovered on the continent of Europe. However, by the end of the eighteenth century, Great Britain was the most important producer of tinplate in the world. At first, it involved the application of a tin wash on thin sheets of iron. Later, the wash was applied to thin sheets of steel.

The process of creating tinplate required iron bars, which came from the ironworks further east in South Wales. These were created by forging. Milling was the process by which the bars were rolled into thin sheets and then the final process was tinning, which gave the sheets their protective coat of tin.

By the time the first tinplate works opened in the Lower Swansea Valley in 1845, the forging process had largely come to be undertaken in-house, and the new works, which were owned by Hallam & Company, included forges and puddling furnaces, as well as the machinery needed for milling and tinning.

Another eleven tinplate works were opened in the valley. The openings came in groups, which reflected the cyclical nature of the demand for tinplate. Most of the Welsh production was destined for overseas, especially to the United States of America.

The second tinplate works was the Landore Works, which opened in 1851. Then, at the end of the decade, demand was rising, partly as a result of the Crimean War, and three more works opened – at Cwmfelin in 1858, Beaufort in 1860 and Cwmbwrla in 1863. There followed a downturn in demand following the outbreak of the American Civil War, when the American economy fell into recession.

Demand rose again once that war was over, and the Worcester Works then opened in 1868, followed by the Morriston Works in 1872 and the Dyffryn Works in 1874. Overproduction led to a fall in prices, with a consequent lack of interest in investing in tinplate during the mid-

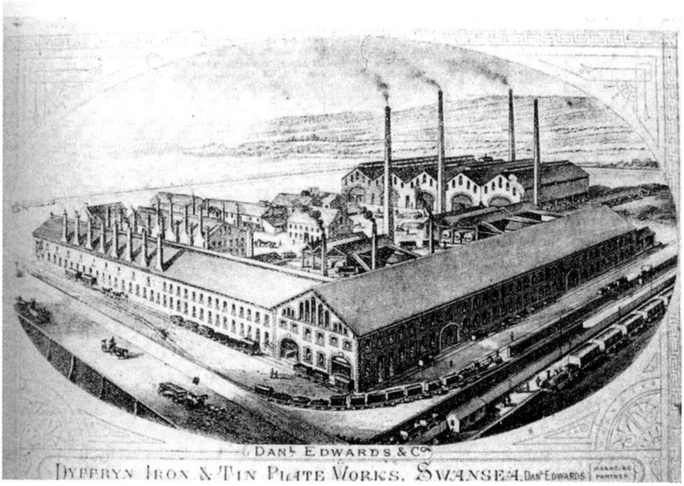

Dyffryn Tinplate Works, Morriston.

1870s. By 1879, though, confidence had returned and the Midland Works opened in that year. The following year saw the Aber Works open, and the final site to be opened in the Lower Swansea Valley was at Birchgrove, also in 1880. Two further works did open, but not in the valley. The Baldwins Company opened works at the King's Dock in 1909 and then the adjacent New Elba Works in 1925.

Welsh tinplate was acknowledged as a superior product, and its success around the world was as a result of its unequalled reputation. In the USA virtually half of all the tinplate used came from Wales. It was especially useful in meat packing, for making oil drums and petrol cans, and for domestic items. However, its success was very nearly its downfall. American producers began to clamour for some support for their own tinplate. The result was the McKinley Act of 1890, which imposed a tariff on all imported tinplate.

The impact on the Welsh tinplate industry was dramatic, with production falling by just over 20 per cent across the 1890s. This had three effects, as it sent the industry into depression. Firstly, there was a rise in unemployment amongst tinplate workers, leading to greater poverty. Secondly, some Welsh industrialists tried to set up tinplate works in the USA, so as to be within the tariff regime. Lastly, skilled Welsh tinplate workers left to live in the USA and work in the American tinplate industry, where their skills would be at a premium. The last two would have a serious effect on the tinplate industry in Wales, as both capital and a skilled workforce would be needed when the turnaround came.

This did eventually come when, after 1898 things began to improve, and by 1902 the level of production was back at its level of ten years before. New markets had been found in Europe, the Far East and the British Empire. The USA, however, remained the biggest market for Welsh tinplate.

Two men stand out in the history of the tinplate industry in Swansea. They were contemporaries, both being born in 1835 and dying in 1915. John Jones Jenkins was born in a cottage in Clydach and Daniel Edwards in Morriston, the son of a stonemason. They must both have shown early promise and received an education, as Jenkins became the manager at Hallam's Upper Forest Works in 1858, and then in 1859 set up his own tinplate works, the Beaufort Tinplate Works on the site of the old Fforest Copperworks.

Jenkins actively pursued the building and promotion of the Prince of Wales Dock. Opened in 1882, this dock meant that Swansea eclipsed Liverpool as the foremost port for the transhipment of tinplate. He also supported and encouraged the opening of the Swansea Royal Jubilee Metal Exchange in 1887. Again, Liverpool lost out to this new trading centre, which became the main exchange for metals in the country. Jenkins became involved in local politics and he was Mayor of Swansea on three occasions. He also sat as MP for Carmarthen, and was created Lord Glantawe, with a seat in the House of Lords, in 1906. A great example of a man from humble beginnings being able to advance economically and socially to the highest levels.

Daniel Edwards was the son of a stonemason, born in Morriston, and himself a stonemason in the early years of his working life. He became an employee at the Hallam Works, and then worked for John Jones Jenkins at the Beaufort Works. In 1868, in partnership with two others, he formed the Llansamlet Tinplate Company, building the Worcester Works, which opened in that year. Five years later, in 1873, he formed his own company and opened the Dyffryn Works in Morriston. He was closely involved in the building of the Tabernacle in Morriston, the construction of which he supervised.

It is mildly diverting to wonder what the relationship between these local captains of industry would have been like. They probably met fairly frequently, socially and at the Metals Exchange. Perhaps they were close friends, united by a common interest in the tinplate industry? Maybe they were just distant colleagues, merely on nodding terms? We can but speculate.

The adoption during the 1880s of steel rather than iron as the base for tinplate brought to Swansea a completely new industry: Siemens' open-hearth steel making. There were two different processes for making steel, both developed in the nineteenth century and both with their respective advantages. Siemens had developed his open-hearth steel-making process during the middle years of the century, taking out a patent in 1867. Bessemer's process was cheaper, but the steel produced was less suitable for rolling. It did not require complicated machinery, so it was cheap to establish as a process. Bessemer's steel found its market in steel rails and similar heavy-duty applications.

The mild steel produced by the Siemens' process was ideal for the tinplate industry and was quickly adopted. As it was superior to forged iron, it revolutionised the tinplate industry. The sheets of steel were smoother than rolled iron, and therefore required less tin to cover them. This, in turn, was reflected in lower costs. Also in 1867, Siemens opened a steel plant – the Landore Siemens Steel Company – just to the south of the railway viaduct. It began production in 1869, and moved to a new site across the river in 1871. From 1875, the production of this plant was almost exclusively sold to the tinplate manufacturers

Other steel manufacturers soon joined in, each producing steel by the open-hearth process. Gowerton, Llanelli and Birchgrove in 1880, Cwmbwrla in 1882, Cwmfelin in 1885 and Upper Forest in 1886.

After the Second World War, the tinplate industry was modernised, with the introduction of the continuous hot strip mill. Demand for steel produced by the open-hearth method declined and the last place in Swansea to include open-hearth steel production was the Dyffryn Works, which closed in 1961.

OTHER METALS

Various other metals produced in Swansea included arsenic, silver, gold and nickel. Arsenic was produced by extraction from copper ore, and there were dedicated arsenic works in the Clyne Valley. Again, this was a good site as there were coal mines in the area, so the coal needed did not have to be transported very far.

Gold and silver were by-products of the copper-smelting process. The Hafod Works carried this out from about 1850 and L. Llewellyn Dillwyn smelted silver at Landore for several years from 1853.

Both cobalt and nickel were produced at the Hafod Isha Works. H.H. Vivian set up a separate company to undertake this work, launching it in 1855.

5

COAL MINING

THE COAL INDUSTRY IN THE SWANSEA AREA

Swansea had become the principal centre for metallurgical industries, with a worldwide reputation, because of its natural resources. The abundance of water and coal, the existence of a natural harbour and a navigable river, a skilled workforce and also, it has to be said, men with true entrepreneurial spirit, although some of these had been drawn by the natural resources, meant Swansea had many advantages.

Perhaps the main one of these was the existence of easily accessible coal. Coal had been mined in the area since medieval times, and had been used for domestic fuel and the burning of lime. In the sixteenth century, the export of coal from the port at Swansea placed it in third place amongst coal-shipping ports, after Newcastle and Sunderland. Swansea's main outlet was France, followed by the Channel Islands and the west of England. Very little coal from the area was used locally.

Local landowners controlled the mining of coal, seeing it as just another product of their estates. The main coal-producing landowners were the Mansels of Briton Ferry. Also important were the Dukes of Beaufort, who, as Lords of Gower and Kilvey, held the mineral rights across the common land and copyhold land in the lordship. This meant that industrialists wishing to obtain coal for their smelters and forges had to obtain leases from the landowners or the lords.

With the development of steam engines for pumping water out of collieries and powering machinery, demand for coal grew even more. Pumping engines of this sort, developed by Newcomen, were in use by Thomas Mansel from 1720 and James Griffiths in 1731. Wooden wagonways for moving coal were in use on the Neath Estate of Sir Humphrey Mackworth, and it is likely that the Mansels utilised them too.

Thus, the coal industry in the Swansea area was well established by the early years of the eighteenth century, producing some 30,000 tons of coal per year. This had grown to some 300,000 tons per year by the end of the century, the increase due in large part to the growth of copper smelting.

Chauncey Townsend, who had begun his career in Swansea in copper smelting, had taken out a lease in order to mine coal but soon realised that coal was a more profitable business to be involved in and gave up his copper-smelting interests. His descendants, the Smith family, became important proprietors in the coal industry.

Lockwood, Morris & Co. also took out a lease to mine coal on the Duke of Beaufort's Estate. As a result of this arrangement, coal mining on the western side of the Lower Swansea Valley was mostly carried out by two producers. John Morris, the second of that name, and his Penvilia Vein Company worked the Beaufort lands and Calvert Richard Jones, who held the Pentre Estate. Also active was the last of the so-called squire coal owners, Richard Mansel Phillips, who was working the coal under his estate, which today we know as Manselton.

Whilst a couple of industrialists moved out of copper smelting and became coal owners, the Vivian family very much wanted a supply of coal that they controlled, so as not to depend on another supplier. John Vivian had set up his copper-smelting works at Hafod in 1809, and had to wait thirty years before he could acquire coal holdings. In 1839, the Penvilia Vein Company was in need of additional capital to bring new areas into production. When it failed to raise this money, John Vivian established the Swansea Coal Company in partnership with Williams Foster & Co. of the Morfa Copperworks. Together, they took over the leases of the Penvilia Vein Company. Over the next few years, they also took over leases held by John Morris, and thus became one of the largest coal companies in Swansea.

By the end of the nineteenth century, the coal industry in Swansea had shrunk to a negligible size. The emphasis had switched to the western edge of the coalfield, as the collieries in the Lower Swansea Valley had become depleted. There was still coal to be found in some of them, and there were times when it was economic to work those remnants, but much more productive collieries could be found outside Swansea, in the Gorseinon area, around Fforestfach and Cockett, plus those in north Gower, the Clyne Valley and Dunvant. These areas grew in importance from about 1850 and, of course, by then the coal could be moved by rail.

The other major coal owner in the Swansea area in the nineteenth century was John Glasbrook. Born in Llangyfelach in 1816, he was in his late twenties when he opened two collieries in the Cockett area. He also took the lease on the Duke of Beaufort's Trewyddfa undertaking in 1854. He took over the Garngoch collieries where, in 1878 coal was discovered. Garngoch No. 1 came into production in that year and Garngoch No. 2 followed in 1884. This became, in time, the largest of the collieries in the Swansea area, employing 520 men. However, the relative size of the Swansea coal-mining industry can be judged by the fact that this colliery only ranked at 109 in size in the entire Glamorganshire coalfield. John Glasbrook died in 1887, but the business continued under the control of his sons, who called the business Glasbrook Brothers.

Today, of course, there is very little evidence of the coal-mining industry in the Swansea area left. Such intensive working over some 700 years was bound to leave the collieries exhausted and the coalfield uneconomic. Before the First World War, when demand was high, thin or deep seams were worth being given the resources to be mined. Once the demand dropped though, in the 1920s and 1930s, there was no point in pursuing the elusive coal.

From 1925, when the Vivians folded their remaining interests, the pumping of water from the remaining pits on the western side of the Lower Swansea Valley halted, and the pits flooded and were abandoned. Llansamlet Collieries Ltd continued to work a few pits on the eastern side of the valley until 1930, and some of the small pits in north Gower carried on until just before the Second World War. One active pit remained in production until 1965, and that was Felin Fran, which had been sunk in 1931 to take advantage of a seam of coal in north-east Swansea.

6

SWANSEA DOCKS

SWANSEA HARBOUR

As we have already seen, the harbour at Swansea was one of the factors in its success. At first, ships moored along the riverbank beneath the castle walls, and later, a town quay was built. The river was navigable for at least 3 miles upstream, so ships were able to dock beyond the actual harbour itself. However, these vessels had to be of a shallow draught, as there was a 9ft-high barrier of sand and gravel across the mouth of the river.

This did not seem to hamper the development of the port. Exports from the port included coal, culm, livestock, butter, cheese, leather and cloth. Imports into Swansea included fruit, grain, wine and pottery, amongst other things.

The busy medieval port did face certain problems, however, mostly resulting from the natural silting of the harbour and the actions of those traders who dumped their ballast into the river. There was a risk that the harbour and the river mouth would become choked, preventing ships from tying up or continuing to the quays further upriver.

In the middle of the sixteenth century, some action was taken to address the problem by making it unlawful to dump ballast anywhere other than at the coal-loading quays or the town quay. The corporation also appointed an official called the layer keeper, whose job was to ensure that any craft laid up on the riverbank after the tide had receded were safe and would suffer 'no strain or damage'.

The corporation had also been active in the sixteenth century in providing their own quays. This continued in the seventeenth century, with the result that there were several municipal quays. The corporation also leased sections of the riverbank, at advantageous rents, to enable private individuals to build their own docks. The eighteenth century, however, found the corporation undertaking much less of this work, and leaving the construction of wharfs and quays to the entrepreneurs who were rapidly developing Swansea's industrial heart.

There was some disquiet in the town amongst the merchants and industrialists that the corporation was no longer doing enough to improve the harbour. In 1768, a public meeting was held to discuss ways of carrying out the necessary improvements, and although it was agreed that using lighters and barges to unload the copper ore ships in the roadstead outside the harbour would partly solve the problem, this was not enough, and proved costly.

The improvements needed to bring the harbour up to the required standard were staunchly opposed by Gabriel Powell, the steward of the Duke of Beaufort, who was the lord of the borough. Powell wielded great power in Swansea, largely through his forceful personality. There were two reasons for his opposition. It is likely that he preferred the town to become a fashionable seaside resort, and trends in this direction were already taking place. Secondly, he feared that the administration of the harbour by an independent body set up by Act of Parliament would lead to a loss of revenue for his lord.

In 1787, another meeting was held to discuss harbour improvements and this came before the burgesses in

Cartoon of the Swansea Corporation meeting at which Charles Collins lost his wig, 1787.

November of that year. Powell again expressed his strong opposition to any action, saying, 'If any act be passed by Parliament to carry the said resolutions into a law it would be very prejudicial to this Town and Borough, and may tend to the manifest destruction of many of our most valuable rights and privileges'. The argument between those in favour of improvements, led by a burgess named Charles Collins, and those opposed, led by Powell, became heated. Tempers flared and Collins was knocked to the ground, kicked and had his wig torn off. Powell eventually won the vote, once things had calmed down, by ten votes to five.

Gabriel Powell died in 1788, and, by 1789, the corporation felt that it was time for co-operation rather than conflict. They proposed opening a subscription to cover the cost of bringing in a surveyor to examine the harbour and suggest ways of improving it. By 1790, just one year later, the corporation had changed its mind. They now favoured promoting an Act of Parliament, and this was successful. The Swansea Harbour Act came into force in 1791 and created a Board of Trustees to administer the harbour.

The trustees who were appointed to the Harbour Trust included the chief agent of the Briton Ferry Estate; Sir Herbert Mackworth, the industrialist, of Neath; an agent of the Duke of Beaufort; and twelve persons:

> ... to represent the interest of the present and future proprietors and lessees of Collieries, Mines and Minerals, and of Persons engaged in Copper Works, Potteries, Salt Works, or any other works and manufactories whatsoever within the said River, Port and Harbour of Swansea, and the owners of ships and vessels frequenting the same.

Changes in the number of trustees were made in the 1804 Harbour Act, again in 1836 by another Swansea Harbour Act and once more in 1854 in a further Act. This last Act set the number of trustees at two, nominated by the Lord of Gower – in practice, his steward and his coroner. Also, the chief agent of the Briton Ferry Estate, nine representatives of the Corporation of the Borough of Swansea and twelve representatives to act on behalf of trade, industry and shipping in the town, joined the board.

In 1794, the trustees asked Captain Joseph Huddart, a renowned marine surveyor, to report to them on the condition of the facilities at the harbour. He made it clear that the priority should be the removal of the sandbar and the construction of two piers, one on either side of the river mouth, so as to prevent further silting. Whilst the trustees agreed with Huddart and adopted his plans, they were very slow to implement the recommendations, and it was 1810 before the dredging and the building of the piers was completed.

The 1791 Act had also given permission for the construction of a 'float' or wet dock, but this was ignored by the trustees, even though Huddart had recommended suitable potential sites. Bristol built a floating dock in 1809, Llanelli in 1828, Cardiff in 1839 and Newport in 1844. At Swansea, however, progress towards a floating harbour was painfully slow. Thomas Telford, the engineer, prepared a report in 1827 in which he stated:

> The Harbour of Swansea is, in my opinion, singularly well situated for being rendered capacious, convenient, and safe, but that this can only be effectually accomplished by converting both the river and the harbour into floats, totally independent of each other, and yet so as to be occasionally connected.

The trustees were a long time in adopting these proposals, and it was only after pressure from J.H. Vivian that they adopted a plan for a floating harbour that had been submitted to them by Jesse Hartley, the Chief Engineer of the Liverpool Dock Company.

There were yet more delays before work started on the project in the late spring of 1840. The plan required the creation of a new cut, which would leave the curved element of the river intact and once lock gates had been fitted, ready to be the new floating harbour. The new cut straightened the river, and although it was at first intended to drain waste water, in 1843 the trustees changed the plan to make it a tidal cut that could be easily navigated by ships heading upriver. 'The Float', so called as ships could now stay afloat whilst being loaded and unloaded, rather than have to be laid up on the riverbank, was opened in 1852.

The slow progress of work on creating and opening the new cut and float – more than sixty years after the initial Swansea Harbour Act that gave permission for the work to be undertaken – meant that other plans had been developed. These were first aired in 1840, and in 1846 the Swansea Dock Company was formed to erect a floating dock on the Burrows. This was close to the fashionable residential area of Swansea, and there was opposition from those who felt their access to the sands and sea would be compromised.

Parliamentary permission for the scheme was obtained, however, in 1847, but actual work did not begin until 1852. The scheme was dogged with bad luck. Two strikes by labourers took place in 1853 and 1854, then in 1855 funds for the project dried up and work was halted.

At this point, the Swansea Harbour Trust came to the rescue and offered to buy the company and the permission to build the float. After some wrangling, the sale went through, and the trustees were able to get further parliamentary permission in 1857 to complete the works. The new facilities opened in 1859, and were named the South Dock, whilst the first float that had been created out of the bend in the river was named the North Dock.

THE TENNANT CANAL

In 1693, an enterprising fellow by the name of Daniel Fabian left Llanrhidian and took a farm on the eastern side of the mouth of the Tawe where an inlet formed a natural bay. Consequently, the little bay was given his name, becoming Fabian's Bay. Adjacent to this, Mr George Tennant, a barrister with considerable commercial nous, took over the Lanywern Canal in 1816, enlarging it and extending it to link the estuary of the River Neath with the estuary of the River Tawe. Thus, Tennant Canal came into being.

Its intended use was the carrying of coal into Swansea Harbour from the Vale of Neath. The site where the canal ended was furnished to provide a 'little docks and shipping place'. A hotel was also built, which necessitated the clearing away of the medieval chapel of St Thomas the Martyr. The whole area became known as Port Tennant.

In 1852, a French mining engineer named Charles Lambert arrived in Swansea and opened a copperworks alongside the Tennant Canal. He had spent a few years in Chile, ultimately owning copper mines there. Ships from Swansea were sailing to Chile to pick up copper ore and carried Welsh coal on the outward journeys. Lambert realised that by using this coal he could partly smelt his ore into regulus and so ship it back at less cost. He visited Swansea around 1840 and established a trading relationship with Henry Bath & Sons, who were a shipping firm. He then established his smelters in Chile.

In a classic example of vertical integration, Lambert then returned to Swansea and established a copperworks alongside the canal in Port Tennant. He now owned the process, from mining the ore to smelting the regulus and finally producing the copper ingots. His works at Port Tennant covered a 12-acre site, which meant that there was limited space when the Harbour Trust wished to build the Prince of Wales Dock on the east side of the river. (Please see Chapter 7 for more about the Tennant Canal.)

THE PORT OF SWANSEA

By the 1860s, therefore, the port of Swansea comprised the North Dock, with its basins, the South Dock, with its basins, the New Cut, which straightened the river, plus the Eastern and Western Piers. There were also some quays.

However, none of this was sufficient to cope with the demands that were being put upon the port. More (and bigger) ships were seeking to use the facilities, and more tonnage was being shipped in and out of the port. Tinplate, galvanised sheets, coal, and patent fuel were amongst the cargoes being transported. Imports of timber for pit props, food, clothing and, of course, copper ore dominated the manifests of ships arriving at Swansea.

By 1874, another Swansea Harbour Act had made its way through Parliament, granting permission for the construction of a new dock on the east side of the river where Fabian's Bay sheltered vessels. This was to be the Prince of Wales Dock, as suggested by the consulting engineer, James Abernethy, whom the trustees had retained to advise on the development of the harbour.

Work started on building the dock in 1879, and it was far enough advanced that the Prince of Wales officially opened it in 1881. In June 1882, the work was completed, and the dock was opened to shipping.

It is worth noting that the harbour at Swansea also contained nine dry docks, all of them in existence before 1899. A tenth, initially Palmer's Dock but then renamed the Prince of Wales Dry Dock, also survived. The Duke of Edinburgh Dry Dock is a much more recent addition.

Swansea was never a major shipbuilding centre. Going back to the eighteenth century, wooden ships were being built by the Squires family, John Mills and Charles Llewhelling, who was succeeded by his son, George. Nineteenth-century shipbuilders included John Tucker and a firm called Meager & Richards.

In the early years of the nineteenth century, shipbuilding in Swansea decreased, but perked up again from the 1850s, when the Richardsons, a merchant family involved in the copper ore trade who also owned ships, increased their shipbuilding activities. They built several of the wooden barques that carried copper ore from South America into Swansea.

From the mid-1870s, though, wooden shipbuilding had pretty much ended in the port and only steamships made of iron continued to be built, albeit they were small in size. The wooden ships owned by the Swansea shipowners mostly came from the North Devon ports such as Bideford or, more importantly, given the numbers involved, from the Canadian Maritime Provinces.

William Richards, a leading shipbuilder on Prince Edward Island, hailed from Swansea, with his brother, Thomas Picton Richards, being a shipowner and broker in the town. Picton Richards began to bring the ships that his brother built into his Swansea fleet, and although they were made of softwood, their cheapness attracted the attention of other shipowners. This led to more Canadian-built ships being bought and added to the Swansea fleets. In fact, in 1876–77, of the 263 ships listed as owned by Swansea shipowners, 112 were built in Canada – just eleven were built in Swansea.

Wooden sailing ships tended to be preferred for the carrying of copper ore, which explained their predominance amongst the ships based at Swansea. Swansea was a major ship-owning port, with a long list of registered ship owners. Many owned just one ship, but others maintained small fleets. However, few of them relied just on the ships they owned for their income. One was a ship's chandler, another was a chronometer maker. Several also built ships or repaired them in their dry docks.

The growth in the quantities of cargo being shipped through the port, and the growth in the size of the ships carrying those cargoes, meant that the Prince of Wales Dock was out of date before the work actually began on its construction. Whilst it did relieve some pressure on the port and provided additional facilities, it was soon functioning at capacity. More dock space was needed!

To provide this, a dock extension was completed in 1898. This enabled Swansea to participate in the newly developing 'liner' trade. Calling regularly were the 'China' boats run by Alfred Holt and the China Mutual Company with their distinctive blue funnels. Others included Williams, Torrey & Field with their two lines – the Atlantic Transport Line and the Manhanset Line. There were Cunard boats sailing to the Middle East and the Mediterranean. The Harrison Line, the Ellerman Line and the Strick Line were also calling at Swansea. We can also add the Pacific Steam Navigation Line and the Bristol City Line. Smaller companies ran coastal services, too.

It seemed that the port was just getting busier and busier and the capacity and the facilities just kept falling short of what was required. A bold move was needed, and it came when the Swansea Harbour Trust came under the chairmanship of Griffith Thomas from Neath. With financial backing from the Swansea Corporation, he set about the planning and construction of Swansea's fourth dock.

Luck played a part in this planning, as it was necessary to find a site for this large undertaking. With the copper-smelting industry suffering something of a decline at the end of the nineteenth century, the Lambert family's copperworks at Port Tennant was a less attractive business. Griffith Thomas took the initiative, negotiated with the Lamberts and successfully managed to purchase the site. This opened up space for dock expansion and the works were demolished and the site cleared. In July 1904, King Edward VII came to Swansea to open this new 70-acre dock. It was given the name King's Dock. At the same ceremony, the king knighted Griffith Thomas in recognition of the work that he had done to bring about the provision of this new facility.

The First World War brought about a fall in trade at the docks when the export markets in German, Belgium and Austria were affected adversely. Coal output also fell as men were diverted from the mines to the trenches. So 1918, therefore, was a momentous year because, as well as the signing of the Armistice, the privations of the war years meant that the Swansea Harbour Trust could no longer meet its financial obligations and two receivers were called in to manage the harbour's business.

The other development involved the Anglo-Persian Oil Company, who opened a refinery at Llandarcy. In order to separate the oil tankers from the other shipping using the port, a new dock was created. Opened in July 1920 by Queen Mary, this became the Queen's Dock.

Three years later, the trustees of the effectively bankrupt harbour negotiated with the Great Western Railway for that company to take over the assets of the trust. An Act of Parliament, the Great Western Railway (Swansea Harbour Vesting) Act of 1923, brought about the end of the Swansea Harbour Trust after 132 years of control. The railways of Britain had been 'grouped' in 1922, creating the London Midland & Scottish Railway (LMS), the London & North Western Railway (LNWR),and the London & North Eastern Railway (LNER), in addition to the Great Western Railway (GWR), which remained as Brunel intended but with numerous other smaller companies tacked on.

This continuity made the GWR a strong undertaking, absorbing, as we have seen, a number of docks. They also owned steamer services, particularly to the Channel Islands, bus services and parcel delivery services. The GWR dock system was, at this time, the largest in the world, encompassing most of the docks along the Bristol Channel and others beyond.

In 1928, the North Dock was closed, as the ships coming into the port were now much bigger and it was also old-fashioned in its facilities. The North Dock Basin, which was alongside the Victoria Flour Mill – better known as Weaver's – was retained for the convenience of ships coming up to the mill.

Although the 'Three Nights' Blitz' of February 1941 did enormous damage to the centre of Swansea, the docks escaped with relatively slight damage. Traffic through the docks was reduced but not extinguished. Prior to the D-Day landings, both troops and equipment were ferried into Swansea. Once the liberation of Europe had begun, the docks were in use as a transhipment point for the war supplies needed to support the forces in the war zone. Anti-aircraft guns were positioned near the North Dock Basin and at the Prince of Wales Dock. There was even a Swansea Docks unit of the Home Guard.

After the war and the nationalisation of the railways, the docks came under the auspices of the British Transport Commission, who created a Docks & Inland Waterways Executive to administer day-to-day control. There was not much money available in those post-war years for repairs or investment. However, some modernisation was carried out to electrical distribution systems at Swansea, and pumping machinery was electrified.

Around 1960, with funds a bit more freely available, Swansea received thirteen new electric cranes. A new jetty was built at the entrance to the King's Dock and some of the quays and wharfs were reconstructed. A new dry dock, the Prince of Wales, was constructed by a private company and BP, who owned the Llandarcy refinery, improved and added to their facilities at the Queen's Dock.

There were other improvements during the 1960s, with the most noteworthy being the construction of a roll-on roll-off (ro-ro) ferry terminal at the East Pier. This included a customs hall and reception hall, a car-handling area covering about 5 acres and a hinged ramp. The service officially opened in May 1969, and passenger usage at the port shot up from about 11,000 to 150,000. In 1979, the ferry port was closed as B & I decided to transfer its Irish sailings to Pembroke Dock. A small amount of passenger traffic did continue on an occasional basis, but then in 1987, Swansea Cork Ferries began a new ro-ro service to Cork.

The South Dock was closed in 1969. Again, it was underused and it became uneconomic to continue providing facilities there. The City Council bought the dock with the intention of filling it in and creating a link road across the site. However, the trend towards leisure facilities for the public, led the council to abandon that plan, and instead they decided to create a yacht marina. The dock was cleared of the partial infill that had begun to be deposited there, and the sea was allowed to flow in once more. The result was a 600-berth marina, and the land around was gradually developed with housing, shops and restaurants. A dockside shed was converted into the National Maritime Museum of Wales and a tall residential tower, topped by a restaurant, was built at the western end of the site. At the time of writing, the Meridian Tower is the tallest residential building in Wales and rather dominates the Swansea townscape.

The building of the Tawe Barrage across the mouth of the river has meant that the river is no longer tidal. Another area for mooring yachts has thus been created, and Swansea is gaining a reputation as a centre for sailing activities. This development has not affected the access to the King's and Queen's Dock. In fact, developments there providing container services has ensured the port's future.

The Prince of Wales Dock, on the other hand, has been rebranded as 'SA1', and has seen a change of use to the provision of office buildings, car-sales showrooms and restaurants. At the Fabian's Bay, or western end, the relatively new University of Wales Trinity St David's has announced its intention to build a campus and student accommodation. Further east along Fabian Way, opposite Bay Studios and technically within the Borough of Neath Port Talbot, Swansea University has already built a new campus and blocks of student accommodation.

WEAVER'S FLOUR MILL

Properly titled the Victoria Flour Mills, the Weaver's building stood next to the North Dock Basin and was part of a complex of buildings owned by Weaver & Co. that straddled the road that passed over the North Dock drawbridge. At this point, the road then led on to a bridge across the Tawe that also carried a tramline and a railway line.

The flour mill was both a grain store and a processing plant for imported wheat. The finished flour was then distributed to bakers, both in Swansea and beyond. The building was erected in 1897, having been designed by the French engineer, Francois Hennebique, and was constructed of reinforced concrete. It is claimed to have been the first building in Europe to be made of this material, although there were grain silos in Romania built of reinforced concrete in the years between 1884 and 1889.

The building's importance locally has led some historians to consider that it became a target for the Luftwaffe in the Second World War, and its close proximity to the centre of the town led to the severe bombing that took place in the Three Nights' Blitz of February 1941. The building, however, survived and finally closed in the 1970s. Demolition came in 1984, although many people thought it was too strongly built to be demolished. The North Dock basin was also filled in and the whole site is now occupied by a Sainsbury's supermarket.

7

CANALS

CLYNDU UNDERGROUND CANAL

John Morris was an innovative colliery owner. He introduced wagonways for the conveyance of coal from his pits to the river for onward transmission. He built a stone quay – the first in the Lower Swansea Valley – and had a tipping chute that allowed coal to be brought onto the quay by wagon, then tipped into a broad, shallow boat to be taken downriver to the port or along the river to the copperworks.

The Clyndu underground canal was dug in the 1770s, and was used to enable coal to be carried out of the Craig Trewyddfa pit and along to the copperworks. The canal was 1,000m long, and the boats that were used could hold the equivalent of two wagons of coal, equalling about 4 tons. As other copperworks were opened in the area, Morris was the man with the coal that they needed. To help distribute the coal, he extended the underground canal for another mile on the surface, in 1787–91.

One further innovation by Morris was in 1768, when he built Morris Castle, a block of flats for his colliers. This is one of the first blocks of flats to be built in Britain. The remains of Morris Castle can still be seen on the ridge high above Morriston.

Morriston was another of Morris' bright ideas and was built from 1779 as a community specifically for his colliers and copperworkers. In fact, it was largely built by his colliers and copperworkers, for the scheme at Morriston entailed granting ground leases to workers, who would then build or arrange the building of a house on their plot. The streets were laid out before building began, and the result was a town with wide streets and pavements.

THE SWANSEA CANAL

By 1794, the mile-long Lockwood, Morris & Co. canal had passed to the Duke of Beaufort. That same year Parliament passed an Act granting permission for the construction of the Swansea Canal. An opportune moment for the duke, and his canal, now named the Trewyddfa Canal, was incorporated into the grander scheme.

Once widened and deepened, the Trewyddfa Canal was ready to become a money spinner for the duke, as the Swansea Canal extended some 16¼ miles from the Strand in Swansea to the Lamb & Flag in Ystradgynlais. Just in the middle of this there was a part that belonged to the duke, who charged a toll for any vessels passing through that section.

From its start at the Strand, the Swansea Canal passed through Landore, Morriston and Clydach before going further up the valley to Ystradgynlais. With thirty-six locks, barges could rise 400ft from the lowest point at sea level. Aqueducts were provided to carry the canal over the several tributaries of the Tawe that it was necessary to cross. Along its banks were wharves, to which the colliery wagonways would bring their coal.

The canal was a considerable success. It opened up the upper parts of the Swansea Valley. However, this success only lasted about fifty years, and canals generally lost trade to the new-fangled railways from about the 1840s onwards.

SMITH'S CANAL

We cannot leave discussion of the canals of Swansea without mention of the Llansamlet (or Smith's) Canal. It was constructed in 1783–85, by John Smith, who was Chauncey Townsend's son-in-law. In 1770, he had bought the mansion called Gwernllwynchwyth from a family called Morgan. The mansion had been built during the reign of Queen Anne, and became the seat of the Smith family and their main residence.

Smith invested quite heavily in the Llansamlet coalfield and made it a great success due, in no small part, to the construction of the canal that bears his name. The canal led from the collieries down to the smelters at Foxhole, and then on to the wharves that lay further south.

The lease of the Llansamlet collieries was transferred to a London lawyer named John Scott, and in 1817 he sank Scott's Pit. This became productive in 1819, and the pit boasted an engine house, which was used for both winding and pumping. He also laid a tramroad, which ran parallel to the Smith's Canal. Like the canal, the tramroad terminated at the Foxhole Wharf, and was known locally as Scott's Railway, and indeed a steam locomotive ran on this railway. Although it was probably a locomotive built by George Stephenson, it proved to be somewhat unreliable. As a result, the ultra-modern was replaced by the ancient and the steam locomotive was replaced by oxen to haul the wagons of coal.

THE TENNANT CANAL

The story of the Tennant Canal begins with its predecessor, the Glan-y-Wern Canal. This was built in 1790 to link the colliery of Richard Jenkins at Glan-y-Wern with the River Neath at an inlet then called Trowman's Hole, but later better known as Red Jacket Pill. Jenkins unfortunately died on the same day that he signed the lease from Lord Vernon for the land to build the canal, so his successor at the colliery, a man called Edward Elton, took over the lease and built the canal. It was in use for about twenty years before Elton became bankrupt and the canal fell into disuse.

George Tennant was the son of a solicitor from Lancashire. He moved to the Rhyddings Estate in 1816. He brought a newcomer's eye to the land that he controlled and felt that Swansea offered better port facilities than did Neath. He decided that a canal would be a good way of linking the River Neath with the River Tawe.

Work began in 1817 and was completed by 1818, and it ran from close to the East Pier on Fabian's Bay to the River Neath at Red Jacket Pill. It was built on a grand scale, and could accommodate barges of 50–60 long tons. A range of cargoes were carried, as well as the mainstay of coal, including timber and timber products, bricks and sand as well as iron and fire clay.

However, even with this solid trade, the receipts were not sufficient to make a profit, and Tennant began to look towards expansion. Abandoning the idea of a lock into the River Neath, Tennant pursued the aim of an extension to join the Neath Canal at Aberdulais. This eventually opened, after some trials and tribulations, on 13 May 1824. Its length from the River Tawe to Aberdulais was 8½ miles and it had cost some £20,000. At its opening, it was known as the Neath & Swansea Junction Canal, but the more common name of the Tennant Canal had been adopted by 1845. Tennant also applied his own name to the area where the sea lock accessed Fabian's Bay and he built wharves, calling it Port Tennant, by which the area is still known today.

Unfortunately, Tennant's canal reached Swansea through an area that was going to see massive expansion as the docks were trying to cater for a huge increase in trade. In 1881, the facilities at the end of the canal were destroyed in the building of the Prince of Wales Dock. A new lock was provided to enable boats to reach the waters of Swansea Bay and a new wharf was provided. However, in 1898 when the dock was extended, the Tennant Canal's facilities were again destroyed. New wharves were provided, this time along the southern side of the new extension. No lock was provided at this time. In 1909, a new branch of the canal was built and this included a lock into the King's Dock, where a berth was provided.

By the 1850s, both the Neath and Tennant Canals were facing competition from the railways, especially the Vale of Neath Railway. Although they were not profitable after about the early 1890s, the canals remained open until the mid-1930s and, as both supplied water to local industries, the infrastructure was maintained in reasonable condition.

Road developments in the Neath Valley affected the canals. However, restoration of certain sections has made it possible for canal boats to run pleasure trips, and there is hope that more work can be done to extend the navigable mileage on both canals.

8

RAILWAYS

THE MUMBLES RAILWAY

At the beginning of the nineteenth century, Swansea was still a fashionable seaside spa town with just a handful of industrial enterprises occupying the Lower Swansea Valley. However, the industries were growing, and they demanded coal, limestone and iron ore, all of which were available in the Clyne Valley and around the village of Oystermouth. Getting these materials to Swansea involved loading small boats from the quays at Mumbles and then crossing the bay to the mouth of the River Tawe. Some could be unloaded there, at the developing port, whilst others were taken up river to be unloaded at private quays linked with iron and copper works.

Alternatively, the minerals could be carried by wagon across the sands of Swansea Bay, but only at low tide. However, no road existed between Swansea and Oystermouth, and this inefficient way of carrying cargo over what was a relatively short distance soon became apparent. Discussions began as to how to solve the problem. One suggestion, made by an eminent local colliery inspector, was for a canal. The Swansea Canal had just been opened and was already making a difference to transport in the Swansea Valley, so a canal would have been a promising proposal. However, another suggestion was the building of a railway.

Several examples of recent successful railways already existed. The Surrey Iron Railway Company had come into being in 1801, the Carmarthenshire Railway or Tramroad Company in 1802 and in the same year the Sirhowy Tramroad had been inaugurated.

Wagonways had already been established at a number of the collieries in the Lower Swansea Valley, and some had developed into tramroads. Therefore, there were local examples of the effectiveness of tramroads, and it may have been this that convinced a number of the promoters of a link between Swansea and Oystermouth that this was the best option.

Swansea Corporation expressed no particular preference, and it was in Parliament that the final decision was made. In 1804, the promoters of a railway won the day and 'an Act for making and maintaining a Railway or Tramroad from the Town of Swansea into the Parish of Oystermouth in the County of Glamorgan' passed through both Houses of Parliament.

The Oystermouth Railway or Tramroad Company held its first meeting on 4 July 1804. Matters moved quickly, in no small measure due to the fact that Sir John Morris was elected chairman of the company, and he was keen to see progress. Messrs Homfray, Tappendens and Birch, owners of the Abernant Ironworks in Merthyr Tydfil, were appointed to supply the tram-plates.

In September 1805, work began on laying the track. It was laid in sections, the first being from the bottom of the Swansea Canal along Brewery Bank; the next took the line along the Strand and past the Royal Institution. It was necessary to demolish the Mount and level the ground at that point. From there, the line went across the Burrows and on to Bond Street, and thence across the sandhills towards Oystermouth.

A branch took the line up the Clyne Valley from Blackpill, and at Oystermouth the line turned slightly inland to connect with the limestone quarries above the village. The first goods traffic finally moved along the line in April 1806. The line was then able to do what it had been designed to do – transport minerals to Swansea.

However, one of the original proprietors, a gentleman named Benjamin French, had come up with a rather original wheeze to make some money. He suggested to the management committee that he be allowed to run an alternative type of service on the line – the carrying of passengers.

Meeting on 16 February 1807, the committee accepted his proposal and, on 25 March of that year, the first passengers were carried on the railway. French himself was one of those passengers.

Let us not forget that these were the first passengers to travel on a railway *anywhere in the world!*

However, the Oystermouth Railway & Tramroad Company was finding balancing the books quite difficult. This was partly due to lax financial management, reduced fees being charged to proprietors of the company when they needed to use its services, and the high cost of repairing track when it was flooded by high tides. In some cases, the track had to be re-laid further from the edge of the sea.

As early as 1808, the company had to borrow £1,500. In 1815, the company defaulted on its payments and was dispossessed of its property. In 1816, a new management took over, although Sir John Morris remained on the board. In 1819, he personally took over one of the mortgages the company held, and in 1823, he acquired the others; thus becoming the man in charge.

This did not make the line any more successful, however, and it continued to struggle financially. Another blow was dealt in 1826, when a toll road was built from Swansea to Oystermouth. Described as 'an excellent road', it drew some of the traffic away from the railway. As a result, in 1827, the Oystermouth Railway & Tramroad Company ceased to carry passengers – or much else. On occasion, a wagonload of coal or limestone might make its way along the line, but in reality it was closed.

The Oystermouth Railway & Tramroad Company, however, was still in existence, although no transactions were recorded between 1827 and 1860. All that had changed was the ownership of that company. Sir John Morris had vested his shares to his son, George Byng Morris. He determined to reopen the line, but initially as part of a greater scheme to link the line with the Llanelly Railway at Pontardulais, which would involve extending the existing line in the Clyne Valley to Killay, Dunvant, Gowerton and Gorseinon, and so through to Pontardulais.

Morris registered a new company, together with George Grant Francis, called the Swansea Docks & Mineral Valleys Company in 1855. Also in that year, he re-laid part of the line up the Clyne Valley to Rhyd-y-defaid Colliery, to enable coal to be carried once again.

After relaying the line through to Oystermouth, Morris reintroduced the passenger service. At first, horse-drawn carriages were back in use, but the plan seemed to be to introduce steam traction on the line. The original Act of Parliament had allowed the use of 'waggons and carriages' that could be drawn by 'men, horses, or otherwise'. The 'or otherwise' put the Oystermouth Railway in a particularly advantageous position, as a subsequent Act of Parliament forbade mechanical traction on British tramways, allowing only animal power unless the Act authorising the tramway in the first place allowed mechanical traction. The 'or otherwise' provided this permission.

Morris was not the only one with an interest in the Oystermouth Railway. The aforementioned George Grant Francis was also eyeing up the line, and had already set up a company called the Swansea Improvements & Tramways Company (SITC) in 1873, which replaced the Swansea Tramways Company. SITC was primarily formed to construct a street tramway system in Swansea. It also had the building of a music hall and a pier at Mumbles among its aims. This latter meant they were interested in acquiring the Oystermouth Railway in order to have the means of transporting their customers down to the pier. SITC failed to purchase the line outright, but was able to come to an accommodation with Morris and he did agree to lease them the line where they also managed to negotiate an exclusive contract.

SITC made no secret of the fact that it wanted to run steam trains on the line, but this caused something of an outcry in the town. For many, things were changing too rapidly, and the former 'gay resort of fashion' of the early years of the nineteenth century had become a large, dirty town, with industrialisation pressing in on the eastern and northern sides. The harbour was now one of the busiest in the country, and the streets were bustling with carriages, horses, horse-drawn carts and people. Having a steam railway running through part of the town and along the seafront seemed to be one aspect of progress too many.

The company had settled on engines specifically designed for use on tramways by Henry Hughes at the Falcon Engine Works in Loughborough. In 1876, this new tramway engine was trialled on Leicester's tramway system. Hughes was a quite brilliant engineer, and also a remarkable tactical thinker. By bringing his engine to the Oystermouth Railway, he was able to stage an experiment where he hoped to prove that the engine was not dirty, nor did it produce steam, nor would it frighten the horses. The experiment, held on 16 August 1877, managed to prove all three claims and regular steam-hauled services began on the Oystermouth Railway the following day.

However, things were about to become rather complicated. Back in 1865, George Byng Morris had agreed to sell the Oystermouth Railway to John Dickson, who at that time was running the Neath & Brecon Railway. He wanted to integrate the Oystermouth line with other lines in the area, but the plan failed as he was unable to raise the purchase price. In 1877, however, he reappeared, claiming that he still had an option to purchase the railway through his agreement with Morris. The courts agreed with Dickson and ruled that the railway be put up for auction. On 31 October, the auction took place in London, and the railway was sold for £31,000 to a company calling itself the Swansea & Mumbles Railway Company. It turned out that this company was owned by cronies of Dickson, who was put in charge by them. Thus, there were now two operators, both entitled to run passenger services on the railway.

Dickson, however, now argued that SITC had no right to run steam services on the line and this was his prerogative. The courts upheld this argument too, and SITC was instructed to stop running steam trains. In July 1878, the SITC tram locomotives were withdrawn and Dickson introduced 0-4-0 steam locomotives.

SITC, however, claimed that it still had running powers on the line, using animal power instead. It therefore continued to run a passenger service until October 1878, when another notice was served and SITC reluctantly withdrew its service. Instead of sitting back, however, it went to court and won the right to restore the service. This time, however, after much wrangling, the judgement in its favour required it to run its horse-drawn tramcars immediately behind the scheduled steam services.

Just as traffic on the railway was increasing, and both companies seemed to be carrying increasing numbers of passengers, by 1884, John Dickson sold his interest in the Swansea & Mumbles Railway Company to two local businessmen: Sir John Jones Jenkins and Robert Capper. They, in turn, offered SITC the opportunity to take a lease on the line. This it did, and from July 1885 it was able to run steam trains on the Oystermouth Railway again.

However, this arrangement only lasted a little over six years. In 1889, Robert Capper transferred his interest in the lease to Sir John Jones Jenkins. He then acquired a large financial interest in the Swansea & Mumbles Railway Company. When the lease then expired, Sir John made the decision to take the line back into the company's hands, and reintroduced the steam service – SITC was cut out again, and was singularly unhappy. It took steps to ensure its running powers by bringing back the horse-drawn service.

Dickson, who was still in nominal charge of the Swansea & Mumbles Railway Company, retaliated in various ways, some barely legal. SITC went to court again but, this time, nothing came of the dispute because, on 13 June 1892, John Dickson died.

A year later, on 26 July 1893, a new company was formed, calling itself Swansea & Mumbles Railways Limited. Sir John Jones Jenkins was the figure behind this new company, and it immediately successfully bid for the old Swansea & Mumbles Railway Company. As Sir John had already had a period of uncomplicated relations with SITC, he entered into negotiations with it. The new arrangement involved an undertaking on the part of SITC to convey passengers on the street tramway system to meet specific trains at St Helen's. There were payments to be made to SITC by the railway company, which continued to run steam passenger trains. SITC then withdrew its horse-drawn carriages, which meant 31 March 1896 was the last day on which horse-drawn conveyances ran on the line.

However, in 1889, a new company had appeared on the scene. This company was called the Mumbles Railway & Pier Company, and by Act of Parliament, it was given powers to construct a new section of line from Oystermouth to Mumbles Head and to build a pier there. Although construction began in 1892, due to various delays the work was not completed until 1898.

The company also had permission to extend the line from Oystermouth back to Blackpill, which would mean two separate lines, run by two companies. From 1 July 1898, an agreement that had the force of Parliamentary approval allowed the Mumbles Railway & Pier Company to work the entire line, all the way to Swansea. However, the shenanigans were not yet over.

In 1898, SITC was taken over by British Electric Traction (BET), who had been promoting electrified street tramway systems with some great enthusiasm. BET electrified Swansea's tramways on 30 June 1900. It had already given thought to buying the Oystermouth Railway from its two owners, but was unable to raise sufficient funds to do so. However, they did arrange to lease the line on a 999-year lease, on behalf of SITC. Thus, at the end of the nineteenth century, the Oystermouth Railway was in the hands of a single operator, holding a long lease, securing its future for the foreseeable future.

For the next twenty-nine years, the steam-hauled services on the railway provided transport for thousands of passengers. The Mumbles Railway had become an integral part of Swansea life, with a trip to Mumbles on the train a must-do activity for residents and visitors alike. Frequent services and the ability to add carriages when necessary mean that individual trains could carry hundreds of passengers at a time.

However, the success of the steam trains ultimately was their downfall. It became clear, especially after the First World War, that the steam locomotives needed to be replaced. With BET in charge, it was obvious that electrification would be the favoured option.

Several things happened before electrification could take place. One was administrative, for BET also owned the South Wales Transport Company (SWTC), which provided bus services throughout Swansea, especially to those areas not served by tramways. BET amalgamated the two companies under the South Wales Transport title. Another development was the provision of electricity infrastructure to feed power to the electric cars. To this end, an electricity sub-station was built at Blackpill. It's still there, converted into the Junction Café. New electric cars then had to be ordered. They came from the Brush Electrical Engineering Company of Loughborough, with eleven being ordered first. These were covered, double-decked cars that could carry 106 passengers and were the largest electric tramway type cars built for use in the UK. Finally, as these cars were much quicker than the steam locomotives and would be providing a more frequent service, a system of signalling had to be introduced, especially where there were passing loops.

With everything in place, a date was set for the new electric service of 1 March 1929. The last steam train ran that day, steaming into its shed at the end of the day. The following morning, the first electric car came out to no fuss or ceremony. However, the iconic cars of the Mumbles train had begun their service, and this first one trundled away and into the hearts of Swansea folk all over the world.

The Mumbles Railway provided a frequent and reliable service to the people of Swansea for another thirty-one years. Through both world wars, although possibly more so in the Second World War, it provided solid reassurance that all was well – the Mumbles train was still running, and would run, whatever happened. During the Blitz, residents of the town used the train to escape to the relative calm and safety of Mumbles and beyond. It also took hundreds of young people to dances and entertainments in Mumbles, on the pier and in the cafés of Oystermouth.

In 1954, celebrations were in order as the Mumbles Railway celebrated 150 years of service. There was a procession, with old and current version of the train on display. Local school children undertook displays of dance and gymnastics. There was an exhibition at the Pier Hotel in Mumbles, and a luncheon at the Guildhall to which the great and the good had been invited. Much was said in praise of Swansea and the Mumbles Railway by the chief guests, and outside, along the track, local folk dressed in period costume to watch the procession go by.

In retrospect, the fine words seem hollow now, and it is likely that thoughts of closure were not far away from the minds of the company dignitaries there present. Just four years later, in 1958, SWTC made a bid to buy the railway outright from the two companies who owned it. Both companies considered what was a reasonably generous offer and agreed to sell. The SWTC moved fast once it owned the railway. A month later, an application was made to the House of Lords and the innocuously titled South Wales Transport Bill, which included provision to close the railway, passed its first reading unopposed. The attempt to sneak the business through Parliament, however, came unstuck when two peers realised what was actually happening.

Opposition broke out immediately, and there were many loud voices raised in opposition. Protest meetings were held, petitions signed, letters written to the press and to the company. But to take the fight to Parliament was a different matter entirely. Although the opponents of bill did manage to put some evidence before the House of Lords committee examining it, it was ineffectual as their counsel had quit the day before and the new counsel engaged was not really familiar with the case. The House of Lords, therefore, allowed the bill to pass. Eventually, despite some opposition in the House of Commons, the bill passed all its stages and closure of the line was now certain.

The date set was 5 January 1960. The night before, a private hiring enabled local people to participate in a mock funeral and wake. The day itself brought almost the entire population of Mumbles out of their houses to witness the last trip by a Mumbles train. Invited dignitaries travelled on the train, and a luncheon was again held at the Guildhall.

All that remains today of the cars that ran on the railway is the front cab of car No. 7. All the rest have been destroyed. Whilst there have been rumours that the railway may be revived, nothing has developed into concrete proposals. In the summer months, a little land train runs along the promenade from Mumbles towards Swansea, giving rides to kiddies and their parents. An ignominious end for the first passenger-carrying railway in the world.

THE SOUTH WALES RAILWAY (SWR) AND THE GREAT WESTERN RAILWAY (GWR)

I make no apology for expending a goodly number of words on the Swansea & Mumbles Railway. It was an iconic railway that enhanced the town and its closure was a mistake of mammoth proportions. However, Swansea did have another railway-related claim to fame, as it had more terminus stations than any other town outside London. There were seven in all, including the Rutland Street terminus of the Mumbles Railway. This, in turn, meant that Swansea was being serviced by seven different railway companies.

The first of these to arrive was the SWR, which left the Great Western Railway near Gloucester, crossed the River Severn and then followed the coast to Chepstow, then on to Newport, Cardiff, Bridgend, Aberavon, Neath, Swansea, Carmarthen and Fishguard.

The engineer for this undertaking was Isambard Kingdom Brunel, and the links between it and the GWR were strong. It was built to the same broad gauge as the GWR, a gauge preferred by Brunel. The original route of the railway had not intended to enter the town of Swansea, passing via Landore. However, when the South Wales Railway Act passed through Parliament in 1846, thus allowing the line's construction, a clause was included to build a branch from Landore into the town of Swansea.

Building the railway line involved some major civil engineering work in order to cross the River Wye at Chepstow and again at Newport. Also, the River Loughor and the River Towy further west had to be crossed. However, from our point of view and the history of Swansea, the main obstacle was the River Tawe at Landore. Brunel's solution was a large timber viaduct across the valley at this point. The thirty-seven-span masonry and timber structure carried the railway line over the river, several roads and the Swansea Canal.

Although Brunel designed the viaduct, the job of actually getting it built devolved to his assistant, Lavington Evans Fletcher. Pile driving began in October 1847, and the masonry work for the western abutment in May 1848, so that by 30 May 1850, a locomotive called *Hercules* was able to cross the completed viaduct. The first passenger train from Chepstow to Swansea crossed on 18 June 1850. The total cost of the viaduct was £28,720.

Between September 1886 and October 1869, replacement works took place, shortening the viaduct by using slag from Hafod Copperworks to increase the embankment on the eastern approach. The whole was reduced to twenty-two spans, supported on more masonry piers. Another refurbishment took place in 1978–79 when steel beams replaced the wrought-iron deck girders.

The whole line from Chepstow to Swansea opened officially on 19 June 1850. On that day, the stations at Chepstow, Portskewett, Newport, Cardiff, Llantrisant, Bridgend, Port Talbot (for Aberavon), Neath, Landore and Swansea all opened. At Swansea, there were flags flying and bands playing as the townsfolk welcomed the first scheduled passenger train when it arrived. The occasion was marked by the *Illustrated London News*, who printed a picture showing the scene.

In 1852 the extension of the railway beyond Swansea resulted in stations opening from Llanelly to Carmarthen, and in 1854 those between Carmarthen and Haverfordwest opened. The line reached Milford Haven in 1856. In June 1852, a section of line was opened between High Street Station and the North Dock.

Swansea was now connected to south-east Wales, Gloucestershire, Swindon and London. However, expansion westward did bring a few problems, especially with a railway company that was to feature quite noticeably in Swansea's history. The Llanelly Railway & Dock Company had been formed in 1828, building a dock at Llanelly and a 2-mile-long railway line to link up with collieries north of the town. For the South Wales Railway to progress westward it needed to cross the two lines owned by the Llanelly outfit.

The Llanelly Company thought that having a pair of crossings of this sort in place would compromise their system. They offered to sell to SWR, but the SWR refused. The two companies wrangled for a while, but eventually came to an agreement, and the SWR carried on towards Carmarthen. From 1 August 1863, the SWR was absorbed into the GWR, and in 1872 they took the momentous decision to abandon the 7ft broad gauge and convert to the much more widely used standard gauge.

THE LONDON & NORTH WESTERN RAILWAY (LNWR)

The Llanelly Railway & Dock Company, however, had carried on with their own plans, which involved running their own line to Carmarthen and another to Swansea in 1867. The line to Swansea left the Llanelly line at Pontardulais, which now became a junction. From there, it passed through Grovesend, where a station was only opened in 1910 and closed in 1931, then to Gorseinon, which was opened in 1867, originally as Loughor Common. Thence to Gowerton South, which opened as Gower Road in 1867. Dunvant, opened 1868, came next, then Killay (1867), Mumbles Road (1868), Swansea Bay (1868) and finally Swansea Victoria, the terminus, which opened in 1867.

The Swansea line was sold to the London & North Western Railway in 1873. Thus was established the major alternative route into Swansea, through which it was possible to travel to Shrewsbury via the Central Wales Line. Given that this ran through the western part of Swansea, down the Clyne Valley and then along the foreshore, it was partly responsible for the lack of residential or tourist development along that foreshore. With both the LNWR line and the Mumbles Railway running along the foreshore as far as Blackpill, where the main line turned up the Clyne Valley, and there being a road alongside them, any development had to take place much further back from the shore. This meant that hotels only developed along Oystermouth Road, reasonably close to the town centre. In turn, Victoria Park, the St Helen's estate and Singleton Park had to be passed before coming to the next houses that had been built beyond Ashleigh Road. This lack of development contributes greatly to the grand sweep of Swansea Bay.

At Blackpill, where the line emerged from the Clyne Valley, a bridge carried the railway over the Mumbles Road and over the tracks of the Mumbles Railway. This bridge was one of Swansea's well-known sights, and was much photographed over the years. During the early years of the twentieth century, it was a popular subject among postcard publishers, with its painted advertising legend advising the general public that here was Mumbles Road Station, and from there one could travel to Liverpool, Manchester and the North with ease.

Another iconic bridge stood a little over a mile away, towards Victoria Station. This was the Slip Bridge, a distinctive structure which took pedestrians over the LNWR tracks, the Mumbles Road and over the Mumbles Railway tracks. Situated at the Slip, where it was possible to walk down a slope to get onto Swansea Beach, this was another much-photographed bridge that also appeared on numerous Edwardian postcards. The abutments of the bridge still stand in their original positions, although the metal girders and the footway across have been taken away and placed on the ground near the cenotaph, some distance away. It seems that there are plans to restore the abutments and place a new bridge on them. On the landward side of the bridge there were public toilets and the entrance to Victoria Park.

Fishing from Swansea Beach, 1960.

Between Victoria Station and the South Dock ran a high-level railway line. This had come from the High Street Station site, down past the North Dock, then turned to cross the bottom of Wind Street – many postcards of Wind Street show the line in the distance – then alongside Victoria Station and on to the Paxton Street Yard. Today some parts of the wall with a couple of open arches remain to remind us of what had been there before.

THE SWANSEA VALE RAILWAY (SVR)

Now to the eastern side of the Tawe, and the Lower Swansea Valley, where a purely local railway developed. We have already read about John Scott and the little railway he built, which was designed to carry coal and became known as Scott's Railway. Built between 1817 and 1819, it was, from its inception, designed to allow locomotives to run on it. The original engine proved to be too troublesome, and was replaced by oxen haulage.

When Charles Henry Smith took over the coal interests of John Scott, he obtained a more reliable locomotive, so that by 1833 there was one locomotive running on the line.

With his own collieries becoming exhausted, Henry Smith looked elsewhere, and in combination with others – including Pascoe St Leger Grenfell and Henry Bath – began to open up the collieries around Glais. In 1845, they formed the Swansea Vale Railway, which incorporated the old Scott's Railway that was already being referred to as 'Mr Smith's' railroad.

The chairman of this new company was Starling Benson, head of the Benson family who owned much land on the east side of the Tawe. He had already tried to build a railway along that bank of the river, but had faced considerable opposition. Now, by involvement with the new company, his ambition was realised. By 1849, it would seem, the old railway had been re-laid to contemporary standards and extended beyond Scott's Pit towards Glais.

In 1853, the SVR bought its own two second-hand locomotives, following up with a third in 1855. It would seem that Henry Smith also had some locomotives of his own working on the line. In 1852, they laid a branch across the Tawe from Foxhole to link with the newly opened North Dock for the carrying of coal. This branch line had been authorised by an Act of Parliament that also gave the company permission to carry passengers. The result of this was that the line was extended down to St Thomas, where a terminus station was built, and northwards to Pontardawe.

The passenger service on this line began in February of 1860. Stations were provided at Llansamlet and Glais, with additional ones subsequently being provided at Upper Bank and Birchgrove. In 1861, the proprietors pushed on to Ystalyfera, and then finally to Brynamman in 1864.

A desirable development at this time was the ambition to link Swansea with Hereford via Brecon. To this end, in 1863 a new company was promoted to link the SVR at Ynysygeinon with the Neath & Brecon Railway at Coelbren. Although the SVR was less than keen on this development, as it felt it would adversely affect its traffic, an Act of Parliament created the ponderously titled Swansea Vale and Neath & Brecon Junction Railway (SV&N&BR).

The new company was soon in financial difficulty. It had entered into a complicated arrangement with a contractor named John Dickson, a man we have already met in connection with the Mumbles Railway. Work on the link between these two railways never really got properly started, and so the Neath & Brecon Railway absorbed the new company in 1869 and completed the construction, opening the line in 1873.

The SVR was operational entirely on the eastern bank of the Tawe, but needed to be able to serve the more concentrated population centres on the western bank. Therefore, in the 1871, the SVR laid a loop line which left the original line at Upper Bank, went through Morriston, Clydach and re-joined the main line at Glais. The line crossed the Tawe close to Wychtree Bridge and then crossed back just after passing through Clydach-on-Tawe Station. This line became the main line for passenger trains, with the original main line being used only for goods traffic. Birchgrove Station closed completely at this time, with Llansamlet Station closing for passengers but remaining open for goods.

The SVR had always found itself strapped for capital, and saw that a way out of this problem would be to sell up to a larger company. As a profitable company, with useful links down the Swansea Valley to the docks, the SVR might have seemed a good bet. It negotiated with the LNWR, but it only wanted to complete the Central Wales line, so said 'no'. It ultimately absorbed the Llanelly Railway Company which, of course, gave the company access to Swansea anyway, but from a different direction.

Clydach-on-Tawe Station.

The Midland Railway, however, was much more interested. It already had a presence in Hereford, having a line from Worcester. Successful negotiations with the Hereford, Hay & Brecon Railway (HHBR) brought the Midland Railway to Brecon, and the next logical step was to come to terms with the N&BR and then the SVR.

The SVR was leased to the Midland Railway in 1874, and absorbed completely by it in 1876, when the SVR wound up its affairs and formally ceased to exist. Thus, the Midland Railway achieved a presence in Swansea, with a terminus at St Thomas.

Grouping, where the railway companies of Britain were organised into four new large companies for the sake of efficiency, took place in 1923. Whilst the GWR carried on pretty much as normal and absorbed several smaller companies, the LNWR and Midland Railways were grouped together, with some smaller companies, in the London, Midland & Scottish Railway (LMS). This new larger concern therefore had two terminus stations in Swansea, at St Thomas and Victoria Station.

THE VALE OF NEATH RAILWAY (VNR)

In the 1840s, H.S. Coke, Neath's Town Clerk, began promoting the idea of a railway to connect the town of Neath with Aberdare and Merthyr Tydfil. Whilst we do not need to concern ourselves with the early development of this railway, suffice to say that it had strong links with the South Wales Railway, had Isambard Kingdom Brunel as its engineer, and was built to the broad gauge.

An Act of Parliament in 1847 authorised the building of the line and work began the same year. Reaching Merthyr proved difficult, but Aberdare was an easier target, and the line there opened in 1851.

Reaching Swansea became an urgent goal for the VNR, as access to the port facilities there was necessary for the mines and works in the Neath Valley and beyond. In response to this, the VNR promoted the creation of a separate company – the Swansea & Neath Railway – which built a mixed-gauge line into Swansea.

The VNR absorbed the Swansea & Neath Railway almost immediately. Starting from a new station in Neath, the line terminated at a platform on the viaduct at the bottom of Wind Street. The waiting rooms and booking office were located in the arches beneath the platform.

In order to reach this station, trains traversed a drawbridge over the lock at the North Dock entrance. This drawbridge was the scene of a major accident in November 1865. An engine hauling thirty full coal wagons failed to stop at the open drawbridge and fell into the lock chamber of the North Dock. The driver and the fireman were both drowned.

In 1873, passenger traffic ceased to use the stretch of line leading over the drawbridge and up to Wind Street Station. The station closed in that year and the VNR trains coming from Neath used Swansea High Street Station. This was possible because, in 1865, the VNR was absorbed into the GWR, and so VNR trains could use GWR tracks. Some services were restored to the old Swansea & Neath Railway tracks in 1881, but now used the East Dock Station of the Swansea Harbour Trust's Railway, despite this being particularly inconvenient for the town.

THE RHONDDA & SWANSEA BAY RAILWAY (R&SBR)

This was the last railway company to bring its lines into Swansea. Its purpose was to bring coal from the Rhondda Fawr at Treherbert down to Swansea Docks for export. A rival scheme had been proposed that would have made use of the tracks of the old South Wales Mineral Railway between Glyncorrwg and Neath. However, the scheme that managed to pass through Parliament involved digging a long tunnel that was to emerge in the Afan Valley. From there, the line was to go to Pontrhydyfen, across Baglan Bay to Briton Ferry, then along the coast, initially crossing the mouth of the Neath River by way of a tidal bridge, and thence into Swansea from the east.

There was opposition, especially to the tidal bridge. The promoters therefore shortened the scheme by stopping at Briton Ferry. Subsequently, there was opposition to a tunnel under the River Neath, but the problem of reaching Swansea was eventually overcome by an agreement with the GWR that allowed R&SBR trains to travel over GWR lines from Aberavon into Swansea.

The railway opened in sections, the first in 1885, north from Aberavon. The next, at Treherbert, was in 1888, and the Rhondda Tunnel opened in 1890, and the section from Aberavon to Port Talbot Docks opened in 1891.

Using the GWR lines to allow R&SBR trains to reach Swansea was not such a good idea, and proved disadvantageous to the company. Therefore, they sought permission to build their own line from Briton Ferry into Swansea. This involved building a swing bridge at Neath. The line heading toward Swansea was opened in 1894. Coming into Swansea from the east at Danygraig brought the R&SBR into the Swansea Harbour Trust complex of lines and, for a short time, it used East Dock Station. The R&SBR then built a short stretch of its own line to its own station at Riverside, both line and station opening in 1899.

In 1906 the R&SBR was effectively taken over by the GWR, although it remained a separate company on paper. This move on the part of the GWR was to prevent the Barry Railway doing the same, and thus acquiring access to Swansea and its immensely lucrative coal trade. Owning the R&SBR also made life easier for the GWR in its attempts to build the Swansea District Line, which avoided Swansea altogether, making the routing of elite express passenger trains on the route to Fishguard much easier. The GWR had high hopes of developing a major harbour at Fishguard, and the creation of an Ocean Terminal there to service the luxury transatlantic liner trade.

In 1922, a result of grouping, the remaining shell R&SBR company was absorbed completely by the GWR. In 1933, the Treherbert to Swansea passenger service was diverted to High Street Station and railcars were provided to run from Briton Ferry to the East Dock Station. Swansea Riverside, the R&SBR terminus, was closed and East Dock Station itself closed to passengers in 1936.

NATIONALISATION AND RATIONALISATION

The Transport Act of 1947 nationalised the railways in Britain, which took effect the following year. The impact of this on Swansea was minimal, as the GWR had rationalised much of the infrastructure it had acquired after 1923. The passenger service between Swansea and Cymmer ceased in 1962. Passenger services on the old Swansea Vale Railway lines ceased in 1950. Goods traffic declined, and bit by bit goods traffic ceased, too. The whole of the old SVR had closed by 1983.

Perhaps the biggest change came as a result of the report into Britain's railways compiled by Dr Richard Beeching. His recommendations resulted in the closure of Swansea Victoria Station, and the whole of the line from there to Pontardulais. Swansea Bay, Mumbles Road, Killay, Dunvant, Gowerton South and Gorseinon stations all closed at the same time. The branch from Gowerton to Llanmorlais had closed to passengers in the 1930s and to goods in the 1950s.

Today, a footpath and cycleway follow the track bed from Gowerton South through the sites of Dunvant and Killay stations and down the Clyne Valley, meeting the Mumbles Road almost opposite the Blackpill Lido.

THE SWANSEA VALE RAILWAY SOCIETY

The only heritage railway ever to exist in Swansea was formed in 1985 when the Swansea Vale Railway Society leased a 2-mile stretch of track between Six Pit Junction and Upper Bank. For over a decade, they were able to run some services on the line, and they amassed a sizeable collection of stock. By 2007, however, the depredations of vandalism were taking their toll, and the refusal of the City Council to continue their support meant that the little railway could not continue. The society merged with the Gwili Railway in Carmarthen, and its surviving rolling stock was transferred to Bronwydd Arms.

9

TRAMWAYS

THE SWANSEA CONSTITUTION HILL INCLINE TRAMWAY

Constitution Hill is a steep, cobbled street that runs from Hanover Street up the hill to Terrace Road in Mount Pleasant. Walking down the hill could be treacherous, especially in wet or icy weather. Climbing back up the hill required considerable exertion, but it did wonders for one's constitution – hence the name.

An enterprising company saw an opportunity in providing a short tramway to allow folk to ride up or down without effort. Development of the line began in 1897 and was carried out by the Swansea Constitution Hill Tramway Company.

The consulting engineer was George Croydon Marks, 1st Baron Marks. A loop halfway up the hill enabled two tramcars to pass each other. The winding house at the top contained two gas canisters that operated pulleys to bring the counterbalance tramcars either up or down.

The line actually opened fully on 1 September 1898. The average number of passengers carried each day was about 500. The fare was 1d, so with five staff on duty at any one time there was little likelihood of it ever making a profit. The staff needed were a driver and a guard on each tramcar, with an engineer in the winding house supervising the winding mechanism. Consequently, the receipts never really covered the running costs. The Tramway Company, however, had close connections with the company that was building houses up in Mount Pleasant, so it kept the tramway open until all the houses had been sold.

Closure finally came on 5 October 1901, and the line was offered to Swansea Corporation. They declined the chance, and the cars, machinery and rails were sold for scrap. The winding house, however, remained at the top of the hill in a derelict state until the late 1970s, when the City Council arranged for its demolition as the structure had become dangerous.

SWANSEA'S STREET TRAMWAYS

In the middle of the nineteenth century, Swansea was expanding both northwards, up the Swansea Valley to Morriston, north-westwards to Cwmbwrla and Fforestfach, and westwards through the Uplands and out to Sketty. This area became popular with the wealthier industrialists, who built large houses there. (They are the subject of a separate chapter.)

After 1870, when the Tramways Act allowed the development of street tramways, providing a comprehensive and cheap means of travel within urban areas, a group of local businessmen formed the Swansea Tramways Company. Their whim of providing a system of street tramways in the town, though, came to nought as they were unable to raise the necessary capital, nor undertake the necessary street widening. Therefore, in 1873 a new company called the Swansea Improvements & Tramway Company (SITC) was formed which could undertake to widen the streets and provide tramways, but also was required to provide a music hall and a pier at Mumbles. We have already met this new company when we discussed the Mumbles Railway.

By 1878, the SITC had laid sufficient tracks to provide services to both Morriston and St Helen's. In 1882, they were able to add a service to Cwmbwrla. These were horse-drawn tramcars that had been built in the USA. The SITC was very keen to trial its steam locomotives, and had attempted to do this on the Mumbles Railway but, as we have seen, were prevented from doing so by the courts. Instead, they used them in a trial on the Cwmbwrla route; but they turned out not to be especially reliable.

In 1900, the SITC was bought out by British Electric Traction Company Ltd (BET), who then undertook to convert the system to using electric trams. Thus, Swansea became the first town in Wales to have an electric tramway system. The first four routes to have electric trams were High Street to Morriston; High Street to Cwmbwrla; Alexandra Road to the docks and Gower Street to St Helen's. The first three of these had low bridges, so thirty single-deck tramcars were acquired initially, with four double-deck cars being added a few months later for use on the St Helen's route.

In 1905, Swansea Corporation attempted to take over the SITC, but were thwarted. They did, however, gain the right to build several new lines with running powers vested in the SITC. Around the same time, Glamorgan County Council built an extension northwards from Morriston to Ynysforgan. This was the first part of a planned tramway running to Pontardawe, which was never built. The SITC provided the electric power and the tramcars for the new extension.

Other extensions were added by the SITC as a means of making the system more flexible. From 1913, therefore, there were eight regular service routes plus two other occasional routes. Three of these began at Castle Street, going respectively to Morriston, Cwmbwrla and Brynhyfryd. There were two routes starting in High Street – one to Sketty and the other to St Helen's. There were also routes from the docks to Sketty; Wind Street to Brynmill and St Helen's to Port Tennant via St Thomas. The two occasional routes linked Swansea Market with Sketty and the Albert Hall with Sketty.

There was, over the time that the trams served Swansea, quite a variety of different tramcars in use. Single deck, reduced-height double deck and normal double-deck cars were employed. As the SITC was quite an innovative company, it was always rebuilding cars so that open cars became covered cars, balcony covers were fitted on some and, for a few, total rebuilds took place. The SITC also acquired cars originally destined for Leeds, which began life as single-deck cars, but were then made into double-deck cars. In-house-built cars were supplemented by new trams from dedicated manufacturers. All this led to a variety of tramcars, which brought enthusiasts to Swansea to see and photograph them.

The 1930s saw a waning of interest in the street tramway system nationwide. A number of towns and cities closed their systems, replacing them with buses or trolleybuses. The reason most often cited was that tramways lacked flexibility which could be provided by the use of buses. Swansea's street tramways closed in 1937, and were replaced by a bus system provided by South Wales Transport, which was shortly to become part of BET, too.

10

RELIGION

THE DISSENTERS MAKE THEIR MARK

We have already come across some of the religious Dissenters present in Swansea during the Commonwealth and the Restoration period. During the Commonwealth, the first change that affected ordinary folk in Swansea was the ejection of the Vicar of St Mary's, Morgan Hopkins, and his replacement by Maurice Bidwell. This change was carried out as a result of Parliament appointing men known as approvers, who were charged with promoting the Puritan take on Christianity.

After the Restoration, King Charles II exercised some greater tolerance and passed legislation that permitted ministers from the Dissenting churches to preach at meeting houses that had been licensed for the purpose. The first in Swansea seems to have been in High Street, just above the Town Gate, and was established by the Baptists, led first by Daniel Higgs and then George Denberry.

About the same time, a congregation of Presbyterians established their meeting house at a different High Street location, but its small size soon meant they built a larger chapel near the Bush Hotel. The Quakers also established themselves in High Street, on a site that later became home to High Street Post Office.

Still in the High Street area, a Dissenters' chapel was built in Back Lane in 1717. This was demolished in the next century to allow the building of the old Swansea Central Police Station. The Back Lane Chapel was the venue for John Wesley to preach when he was on one of his regular visits to Swansea, which began in 1758.

There seems to have been some fluidity amongst ordinary Dissenting people, and adherence to a particular persuasion was not always firm. An example of this was William Howell, who initially followed the preacher Solomon Harris at the Unitarian Church in High Street, but later split from the Unitarians to establish his own chapel in Castle Street. Similarly, a congregation of Independents that had been established at Mynyddbach saw a breakaway group establish Ebenezer Chapel, which followed the teachings of John Wesley. Two local men, one from Neath and the other from Swansea, managed to persuade Selina, Countess of Huntingdon, to establish one of her chapels on the Burrows in 1789.

At the top end of High Street there was a mound called Crug-Glas, which was painted with a disreputable reputation as it was the venue for visiting fairgrounds and so had become the haunt of drunkards and other ne'er-do-wells. However, in the face of all the opposition that this hostile audience could muster, Howell Harris chose the site to preach several times. Not only was he jeered and ridiculed, but on one occasion an attempt was made on his life. A pistol was aimed at him by a drunk in the crowd, but it misfired, leaving Harris unharmed.

In the 1780s, David Thomas, a member of the Independent congregation from Mynyddbach, came to live in Swansea and naturally went to the meetings of Independents at the Old Room in Castle Street. After a few years, he found himself disagreeing with certain members of the congregation there and, as a wealthy brewer, had the funds available to build his own chapel at Crug-Glas.

Both Howell Harris and John Wesley remained within the Church of England whilst preaching their beliefs, despite voices from within their own movement demanding that they separate and ordain their own ministers. The Wesleyans did split once John Wesley died in 1791. The Calvinistic Methodists held on until 1811, when they separated from the Established Church. Thus, two new denominations were added to the list of Dissenting Churches.

Doctrinal differences continued to cause rifts in various congregations, resulting in new chapels being built. Often these additional chapels were funded by wealthy local landowners or industrialists. One division, though, which took place after the death of the inspirational pastor Joseph Harris in 1825, was the division of the congregation of the chapel in Back Lane. This chapel had come into being itself as the result of a split in those attending the chapel in Baptist Court. In 1827, the congregation split into an English congregation and a Welsh congregation. The English Baptists built their new chapel on what is now the Kingsway, whilst the Welsh Baptists opted for a site on Prince of Wales Road, opening in 1831.

In 1851 a religious census was carried out in Swansea, to determine the number of places of worship, and the religious make-up of the population. The Church of England had four churches, whilst the Independents had seven, the Baptists had five, the Calvinistic and the Wesleyan Methodists had four each. The Primitive Methodists, Lady Huntingdon's Persuasion, Unitarians, Quakers, Roman Catholics, Jews and Mormons all had one place of worship each.

The Presbyterians gained a place of worship in 1864 when they built St Andrew's Church. An English Congregational chapel opened on Walter Road in 1869, which led to other denominations providing alternative chapels for the English speakers in their congregations.

THE ANGLICANS IN SWANSEA

The fortunes of the Established Church at the beginning of the nineteenth century were low indeed. Swansea's two Anglican churches were in poor states of repair. Congregations were declining, especially after the Calvinistic and Wesleyan Methodists split from the Church. Pluralism was commonplace, with vicars holding more than one living, plus curacies, often a distance away from their main living. At a national level, however, and as a result of governmental pressure, the Church was beginning to make reforming changes. Abuses like pluralism and absenteeism were tackled, and the creation of new parishes, essential when populations were responding to industrial development by moving into new towns, was speeded up.

The Vicar of Swansea from 1813 to 1845 was Dr William Hewson, but he seemed content to carry on much as before, and much hope was placed in his successor the Rev. Robert Shirley Bunbury, an evangelical with plans for the future. However, unfortunately, he lived only a year after his appointment and so his plans went unrealised.

It was as well for Swansea that the next vicar, the Rev. Edward Burnard Squire (1846–76) and the later appointment of the Rev. J Allan Smith in 1885, put two enthusiastic priests into the living at St Mary's. Rev. Squire had enjoyed several exotic careers before being ordained in 1841. He had served in the East India Company, as well as both the Indian Army and Navy. He was the commander of two sloops during the first Burmese War in the 1820s, and acted as an agent in China for the Church Missionary Society. He brought an energy and enthusiasm to his role in Swansea, where he became well known. He urged his congregation, as well as the clergy, to go out and minister to the destitute in the slums of the town. To promote this, the Swansea Parochial Visiting Association was established, and thousands of poor Swansea folk benefited both materially and spiritually.

The other great issue facing the Church was rapid expansion of the urban parts of the town, and how to provide the growing population with the support they needed. The process called 'church extension' was launched in order to build new churches and create new parishes. At Sketty, the Vivians funded the building of a new church, St Paul's, which was consecrated in 1850 and very soon after became a new parish. On Oystermouth Road in the Sandfields, Christ Church was built at the expense of John William Clark, a wine merchant. Consecrated in 1872, it became a separate parish in 1874. In Cockett, St Peter's was built partly due to the largesse of John Dillwyn Llewelyn and was consecrated in 1856 but had to wait until 1878 to become a parish. Near the Uplands, at the top of Walter Road, St James' Church was built in 1867.

This growth in church building during Rev. Squire's vicariate continued into the vicariate of Rev. J. Allen Smith. St Matthew's was built in 1887 and St Mark's, St Thomas' and St Gabriel's all opened in 1888 and 1889. His greatest achievement, however, would be the raising of funds to finance the rebuilding of St Mary's Church in the last few years of the nineteenth century.

It has been suggested that this church originated as a Celtic monastic foundation, if a settlement had ever been in existence on the site before the Norman occupation. Certainly, a Norman church had been built there early in the twelfth century, but it is not known what that really looked like.

On 30 May 1739, the vicar, Charles Davies, was delayed by the late arrival of his barber who was due to administer his morning shave. A large part of the congregation were standing outside the church waiting for him, when, without warning, the roof of the nave collapsed. The tardiness of Rev. Davies' barber, in this instance, undoubtedly saved lives, as the congregation was not gathered inside the church. One fellow was injured, but there were no deaths.

The church building, however, was now in a ruinous state, and it was necessary to carry out quite extensive repairs. St Mary's had been unusual, although not unique, in having its tower separate from its nave. When the contractor chosen to undertake the repair – Thomas Woodward from Worcester – carried out the rebuilding, he linked the tower with the nave, inserting a stairway leading up to a gallery. He also removed the south porch and built a new one at the western end.

Thus the church remained until 1895 when the church was comprehensively rebuilt to designs by Sir Reginald Blomfield. Further repairs became necessary after the Second World War, as the church suffered considerable damage in the Three Nights' Blitz on February 1941. The rebuilding was carried out by Sir Percy Thomas, who used the original plans drawn up by Sir Reginald Blomfield to exactly recreate the 1895 church.

There had been agitation for a number of years demanding the disestablishment of the Church of England in Wales. This was finally enacted in 1922, with administrative changes following in 1923. Swansea had always been part of the Diocese of St David's, indicating its attachment to West Wales rather than South Wales. In 1923, this huge diocese was split, with Swansea becoming part of the new Diocese of Swansea and Brecon, which incorporated Gower, Swansea and a large part of what is today Powys, stretching up to English border. The church in Brecon was chosen to be the cathedral, most likely due to its central position.

The Swansea Devil

Before moving on from the history of St Mary's Church, it is necessary to include a description of an iconic Swansea figure and the traditional story that surrounds him. In the run-up to the rebuilding of St Mary's Church in 1895, the commission was put out to tender. A number of architects submitted plans, including one local architect who was especially confident of success. In the event, Sir Arthur Blomfield was the chosen architect, much to the chagrin of the local man.

A few years later, the local architect was given another commission to build some brewery offices on the site of a row of old cottages opposite the church. With this, he devised a plan to get his revenge on the church fathers who rejected his plan. Once built, he topped the brewery offices with a carved wood effigy of the Devil – 'Old Nick', as he became known in the town. The figure was placed in such a way that he overlooked the church. Some versions of the story have the architect issuing a curse: 'When your church is destroyed and burnt to the ground my devil will remain laughing.'

Half a century later, the prophecy came true, courtesy of the Luftwaffe and the Three-Nights' Blitz on Swansea. Whilst the buildings all around were destroyed, 'Old Nick' and his brewery building were virtually unscathed. St Mary's was severely damaged, and maybe the following day the Devil on his perch did have a little laugh, although anyone passing by might have dismissed it as a policeman with wind.

St Mary's was subsequently rebuilt, the brewery offices were demolished and the Quadrant Shopping Centre was built on the site. 'Old Nick' disappeared, and was assumed lost, but eventually he turned up in a garage in Gloucester in the early 1980s. He was then returned to as near his old position as possible, high up on the Quadrant roof. There were objections, and he went back into storage for a while, but then, as a result of a public campaign, went up on the roof again. In 2019, the owners of the Quadrant donated him to the Swansea Museum, where he sits on display in a glass case.

THE ROMAN CATHOLIC CHURCH IN SWANSEA

During the time of the Commonwealth, being a Catholic was to bring persecution and a real risk to your life. Being a Catholic priest was even riskier. Swansea provides a footnote to this period of British history in the fate of one Philip Powell who was on board a small boat lying off Mumbles Head. He was arrested on 22 February 1646, suspected of and charged with being a Catholic priest. He was taken to London, and then before a court that found him guilty of the charge and sentenced him to be hanged, drawn and quartered. His execution, at Tyburn, took place on 30 June of that same year.

We do not know whether he was arriving or leaving Swansea, nor do we know who put the finger on him and reported him to the authorities. We do know, though, that Swansea had a very small Catholic community indeed. By the 1760s it had virtually died out, with just one 40-year-old man working at one of the copperworks and a family of six on their way back to France. However, with the growth of industry in the town, and the arrival of workers from outside the area, Catholic numbers began to grow.

Still few in number, priests came from Bristol to minister to them. In 1797, a Jesuit priest named Robert Plowden managed to create a tiny chapel at the Plas, and in 1799 a group of five French Catholics arrived, following the French Revolution. One of these was Abbé Albert Séjan, who built a small chapel in Nelson Terrace in 1810. Its congregation was normally less than twelve. Séjan returned to France in 1814, so the few Catholics still in Swansea had to rely on occasional visits from priests travelling to the town.

Many of the workers who came to find work in Swansea, came from Ireland, especially after the Great Famine of 1845–46. Father Charles Kavanagh had arrived in 1839, so a resident priest was available to these incomers. His dedication earned him a great deal of respect amongst the townsfolk, so much so that when he unexpectedly died in 1856, he was honoured with what amounted to a civic funeral.

The Catholic population of the town was expanding and in 1864 St David's Church was enlarged and a new presbytery built. The bulk of the Catholic population was centred on the Greenhill area of town, and a church dedicated to St Joseph was opened in 1866. In 1873, the Benedictine order arrived to swell the Catholic clergy, along with a group of Ursuline nuns who established a convent at Greenhill.

With the pastoral work of the priests enhanced by these arrivals, a new confidence developed amongst the Catholic population. A new priest, Father Wulstan Richards OSB, came to Greenhill in 1875. He felt that a new church was necessary to serve the growing parish and arranged for St Joseph's to be built at Greenhill. It was designed by Peter Paul Pugin of Pugin & Pugin, the famed architects, and opened in 1888, although construction had not been completed at that time.

St David's Roman Catholic Church, 1856.

In 1987 the Diocese of Menevia was reorganised, and the church at Greenhill was designated the Cathedral Church of St Joseph in Swansea – sometimes also referred to as Menevia Cathedral – on 30 March that year.

11

EDUCATING JACK (AND JILL)

Throughout history, not everyone felt that education for the masses was a good thing. John Glasbrook, the Swansea industrialist, wrote in 1870, 'The working classes have too much knowledge already; it was much easier to manage them twenty years ago; the more education they get, the more difficult they are to manage.'

These words were intended to oppose the setting of a special rate in Swansea to finance a public library. This was the year of the Education Act, which made elementary education compulsory, so Glasbrook's opinions were clearly not widely shared. There had been a Reform Act in 1832, and another in 1867, which increased the number of voters, allowing many more of the 'working classes' to vote. It was felt that a basic education was needed to ensure that these new voters understood their roles and responsibilities.

However, educational provision had existed in Swansea well before the Victorian age, and we do need to understand what went before.

EDUCATION IN MEDIEVAL TIMES

From the time when Swansea was founded, there was a small monastic presence in the town, whose role it was to provide alms, spiritual guidance and some educational opportunities. Local boys showing some ability could enter the monastic life as novices and would have learnt to read and write. There is no concrete evidence for this, of course, but in similar towns elsewhere in Norman-occupied Britain, this did occur.

The nearest monastery to Swansea was at Neath Abbey, so some youngsters may have entered there. However, this would only have accounted for a tiny number of boys. Girls may have had the opportunity to enter a convent, but again this would have been a tiny number, and neither the boys or girls would have come from ordinary homes.

The other education available for boys in the town was to be apprenticed to one of the burgesses and so learn a trade. This was a practical education, but an essential one if the town was to grow. It was also open to boys from the working classes.

EDUCATION AFTER THE REFORMATION

Once Henry VIII had dissolved all the monasteries, so disappeared one source of education for talented boys. Parish priests now were more likely to be involved in providing some basic education, but this would have been sporadic and very much dependent on the abilities and enthusiasms of the priest. It is known that some priests, known as travelling priests, did set up the occasional school, especially in the period after the Civil War. Jobless and essentially without permanent residences, they would take over a room in a building or a church porch and provide some tuition in reading and/or writing for a few pence.

WHAT ABOUT THE POSH BOYS?

Much has been written these days about the influence of the 'posh boys' on government, Parliament and business in Britain. The feeling is rife that Eton- and Oxbridge-educated men run the country from a position of privilege. It was ever thus.

The sons of the nobility, clergy and upper middle-class privileged families have always preferred private education at one of the great English public schools. By following this up with a university education, either at Oxford, Cambridge or elsewhere, they were thereby kitted out to run the country, or, after the rapid expansion of the British Empire, other people's countries. Couple this with the education of girls from similar backgrounds by tutors in their own homes, or by governesses who had been educated the same way themselves, and the elite remain firmly in charge.

Many of the industrialists and entrepreneurs who created Swansea's wealth came from this class. With money behind them, enquiring minds and pioneering spirits, they built the infrastructure that underpinned the Industrial Revolution. They also provided work for thousands of ordinary working-class folk.

It was these men who founded the various intellectual societies that gave Swansea a reputation as an intellectual centre. In 1835, the Swansea Philosophical & Literary Society was formed. It had as its objectives 'the cultivation advancement of the various branches of natural history, as well as the local history of the town', and it also added, 'the extension and encouragement of the fine arts and the general diffusion of knowledge'.

The Royal Institution of South Wales (the building) was opened in 1841. The driving force behind the establishment

The Royal Institution of South Wales, 1850.

of this institution was George Grant Francis, supported by Lewis Weston Dillwyn, John Henry Vivian and C.R.M. Talbot, all Fellows of the Royal Society, and names familiar in the development of industry in the area. Another four supporters were John Dillwyn Llewellyn, William Edmond Logan, John Gwyn Jeffreys and William Grove, all destined to become Fellows of the Royal Society in their turn.

The Royal Institution hosted lectures on a variety of subjects, sponsored some research and acted as a museum. It's greatest coup, however, was to bring to Swansea the meeting of the British Association for the Advancement of Science in 1848. With a solid reputation for scientific research in the area, and the fact that Swansea was, at the time, seen as the principal town in Wales, its choice as a venue seemed perfectly sound. Indeed, the holding of the meeting there meant that Swansea's reputation was considerably enhanced. It was seen as having a notable intellectual pedigree.

Bishop Gore and Swansea Grammar School

But, we are getting ahead of ourselves. This reputation was not won overnight. Some of the credit for turning Swansea into an intellectual haven must go to a refugee from Ireland. Hugh Gore was a parson's son from Dorset, who was educated with a view to taking a post in the Church in Ireland. However, his father's friendship with the Mansel family led him to accept the living of Oxwich.

He was expelled from there at the time of the Commonwealth, and so he started a school in Swansea. This did not last long, and he soon went to a parish in Ireland. There, he obtained preferment to the Bishopric of Waterford and Lismore.

His affection for Swansea was such that in 1682 he founded a school in the town for the free instruction of twenty sons of the 'poorer sort of burgesses'. It was endowed with farmland in Ogmore Vale.

The residence of Bishop Hugh Gore in High Street. He lived there from 1689–91.

The Glorious Revolution of 1688, which brought William of Orange to the English throne, caused some considerable disturbance in Ireland and Bishop Gore fled, returning to Swansea and a house in High Street. In 1691, though, he died, and was buried in St Mary's Church.

The school he founded, however, continued. The appointment of master had been laid down in the founding charter as the responsibility of the descendants of Bussy Mansel, who had been Bishop Gore's friend. Once Bussy Mansel died in 1699, the Swansea Corporation took a sporadic interest in the appointment of the master and the school began to decline. The Rev. Evan Griffith was the last master under the original foundation, and on his death in 1842, the school closed.

Mount Pleasant, 1818.

Onto the scene comes George Grant Francis, whom we have already met. He was given the job of tracking down the heirs of the original trustees of the school. He met with success in South America, tracing one man, named Thomas Gwyn, the heir of the last surviving trustee. With Gwyn's acquiescence, a new scheme was approved to revive the school. A new building was erected on Mount Pleasant and opened on 14 September 1853. The school survived on that site until the Second World War, when bomb damage caused it to close. After the war, it was relocated to a new site in Sketty, and renamed Bishop Gore Grammar School. Possibly the most famous scholar to attend the Grammar School at Mount Pleasant was Dylan Thomas.

CIRCULATING SCHOOLS

As we have already seen, education was largely in the hands of the Church of England, which should have been providing a school in each parish, where a schoolmaster, who would have been licensed by the bishop, taught the ordinary people enough to be able to read the Bible and Catechism. They also promoted in their pupils the benefits of hard work, deference and an unquestioning acceptance of their position in the social order.

There had already been attempts to establish these schools on a permanent basis, and for the regular distribution of Bibles and other religious publications, but with only mixed success. Then, in the early eighteenth century, Rev. Griffith Jones came up with the idea of schools that only functioned in winter months and were staffed by itinerant schoolmasters who would return each year. In Swansea, in 1745–46, it is known that 201 pupils attended.

Schools were also organised on farms in Llansamlet, Pentre Estyll and Olchfa, amongst others. The level of success was due to two factors – there was flexibility in the hours of tuition, and the language used for instruction depended on the language of the community, Welsh where Welsh was spoken and English elsewhere.

These Circulating Schools had their heyday between about 1738 and 1777. As a result, the level of literacy amongst agricultural and industrial workers rose, and also awareness of the arguments being put forward by Methodists and other Dissenters, thus fuelling the religious revolution of the next 100 years.

VOLUNTARY SCHOOLS AND JOSEPH LANCASTER

The Quaker educationalist Joseph Lancaster was not interested in promoting a particular religious outlook for schools, although he was linked with the British Society. He was largely concerned with the organisation of pupils in order to allow for the teaching of the maximum amount of pupils under one teacher. His system was called the Monitor System, and enabled the teacher to train older pupils to a level where they could then teach younger pupils. It proved to be a particularly effective system, and was in use in voluntary schools for many years, even after the Education Act of 1870.

Lancaster's system was adopted early on in Swansea. The Swansea Society for the Education of the Children of the Poor was formed in 1806 as a result of his visit to the town in that year. A boys' school based on his system was opened the same year, with a girls' school opening in 1811. The boys' school was the first Lancasterian school in Wales, and was followed by many more. After 1814, these schools came under the auspices of the British & Foreign Schools Society, who went on to open others, including the Hafod Copperworks School, funded by J.H. Vivian in 1847. These schools tended to be called British Schools to differentiate them from the Church of England National Schools.

Altogether in Swansea at that time there were some fifty-three schools, but, of course, many of them were not necessarily of a good standard. Poor teaching could only be tackled if the training for them was improved. With this in mind, a Normal College for the training of teachers was opened by Dr Evan Davies at Ivy Lodge in Nelson Terrace. It continued there for a number of years until it moved to bigger and better premises on Townhill in 1913.

THE SWANSEA SCHOOL BOARD

The Education Act of 1870 heralded the provision of free but compulsory elementary education for children up to the age of 14. At first, the intention was to fill the gaps that existed in the educational provision provided by those voluntary schools that had been established by the British and National Societies.

In Swansea, a School Board was established in line with the provisions of the Act and, needless to say, John Glasbrook did not become member. The first chairman was Charles Thomas Wilson, a man who wanted to see action in the provision of schools.

The first steps, however, were in taking over the administration of those schools run by the British & Foreign Schools Society. Neither the British Schools nor the Works objected to being taken over by the boards, but the National Schools put up considerable resistance, and remained independent of the board for several years.

New schools were built, including at Pentrepoeth, Plasmarl, Llangyfelach, Ynystawe and Tirdeunaw. As the number of school places needed was still high, the board took the decision to build larger schools on four sites. Terrace Road School was built in 1888, St Thomas School in 1898, Manselton in 1900 and Hafod in 1905. These large, multi-storied schools still dominate their neighbourhoods.

A further complication for the School Board was the requirement to provide secondary-level schools. The Board of Education suggested this in 1882, and in 1883, a Higher Grade School was founded at Trinity Place. In 1894, the boys transferred to a new school in Dynevor Place. A flurry of name changing over the following years ended when the enlarged Dynevor Place building became the Dynevor Secondary School for Boys, and a new building next door became the De-la-Beche School for Girls, which opened in 1929.

The 1889 Welsh Intermediate Education Act established a Joint Education Authority for Swansea. In 1895, the Swansea Grammar School was converted by them into the Swansea Intermediate & Technical School for Boys. The Grammar School was subsumed for a while, but reappeared after the Second World War as Bishop Gore School in Sketty.

The High School for Girls, which was actually a private school, transferred to the new authority and was renamed the Swansea Intermediate & Technical School for Girls – which we probably know better as the now-defunct Llwyn-y-Bryn Girls' School. This amalgamated with Dynevor School in the late 1970s to form a single new Dynevor School which operated on three sites. In addition to the two school sites, classes were also taught in the Old Guildhall building in Somerset Place. Dynevor School was always hampered by the cramped city-centre site that it occupied, and it closed in 2003.

The last of the pre-war secondary school foundations in Swansea was the opening of the Glanmôr Boys' & Girls' School in 1922. Utilising a wooden building on Glanmôr Road that had been an American army camp during the First World War, it became a solely girls' school in 1941. The girls stayed on until 1972, when they transferred to the newly opened Olchfa School.

On 3 September 1970, Swansea City Council introduced a city-wide comprehensive system of secondary education. The 11-plus examination disappeared, as did the grammar school status of a number of schools. New secondary schools had already been built at Penlan in 1956, Mynyddbach in 1959, both being single-sex schools, and at Bishop Vaughan in 1967 as a Roman Catholic secondary school. Cefn Hengoed was added in 1968, Olchfa in 1969, Morriston in 1970, Pentrehafod in 1976 and Dillwyn Llewellyn in 1981 (which is now the Dylan Thomas Community School), both of the last two were opened under the auspices of the West Glamorgan LEA.

Since that time, further new secondary schools have been opened at Bishopston, Penyrheol, Pontardulais and Birchgrove, in the enlarged local authority area that the City of Swansea has become.

HIGHER EDUCATION

Swansea Technical College was admitted into the University of Wales as one of the constituent colleges – the University College of Swansea. Almost immediately, work began on the building of a new college on a site adjacent to Singleton Park. In July 1920, at an elaborate ceremony, the foundation stone of the new college was laid by King George V. The building was ready for occupation in 1923. The nearby

Singleton Abbey in 1881, from the *Illustrated London News*.

Singleton Abbey had already been put to use to accommodate the new college; this had been the home of John Henry Vivian, but after 1923 became an administrative block.

The old technical college, however, retained its identity and remained on its site on Mount Pleasant Hill. Since that time, it has been the West Glamorgan Institute of Higher Education, when it absorbed the old Swansea College of Education – that's the Teacher Training College on Townhill.

When institutes of higher education were allowed to apply for university status, Swansea did just that and became the Swansea Metropolitan University, adding the old Dynevor School buildings as another campus. Further changes have since taken place. The Dynevor campus is now referred to as the Swansea College of Art and, with the other Swansea campuses on Mount Pleasant and Townhill, has joined Carmarthen College and Lampeter University as the University of Wales Trinity St David's (UWTSD).

A new campus – which might be in addition to or a replacement for the existing campuses – is being built in the new SA1 development on the site of the Prince of Wales Dock. Further along Fabian Way, the University of Swansea has built a large new campus, which I mentioned earlier. This is just the latest development for a university which now ranks top in Wales.

12

POSTAL SERVICES IN SWANSEA

The first firm evidence we have of any kind of postal service for Swansea is in 1599, when the courier service that served the Crown created permanent posts. These emanated from London, and two went through Wales: one in the north went to Holyhead; the other, in the south, went to Milford Haven, but passed through Cardiff, Swansea and Carmarthen on the way. There were stables of fresh horses kept at these towns, so the post would have stopped there, and mail would have been exchanged. This service was probably no longer functioning by 1620.

In 1625 Charles I gave Thomas Witherings authority to establish six post routes out of London. None of these came to South Wales directly, as the nearest stopped at Bristol. It seems likely that mail could be sent on from there to the South Wales towns. These posts stopped at the outbreak of the Civil War and the next publicly available post appears in 1652. The post from London seems to have come via Swansea, although evidence for this is scant.

In 1674, the mail route to Ireland was altered, going from London through Gloucester, then to Monmouth, Brecon and Carmarthen. Cardiff and Swansea had to make do with bye-posts from Monmouth, the Swansea bye-post requiring only a letter office in the town, rather than a staging post to supply fresh horses.

Mail coaches were introduced on these routes 100 years later, with additional routes improving the service between Bristol and Swansea. From 1804 this was a daily service and from 1808 the route to Carmarthen also became daily. This was the golden age of the mail coach, and it lasted until 1850.

In Swansea, the mail coaches arrived at and departed from the Mackworth Hotel in Wind Street. It is one of the ironies of history that, in 1898, in order to build a new head post office in Wind Street, the Mackworth Hotel was demolished and relocated to High Street.

One important development during this mail-coach era was the introduction of a direct mail coach to Merthyr Tydfil in 1835. Thus Swansea, the most important town in Wales at this time, had a direct connection with Merthyr Tydfil, the largest Welsh town. Further to this, a direct mail coach was introduced to Llanelli, replacing the horse post that had previously operated over the route.

Then, in 1840, the greatest change to postal services came when the reforms instigated by Sir Rowland Hill introduced the Uniform Penny Postage. The success of this initiative was in large part due to the fact that mail could be conveyed by rail. In Swansea, once the South Wales Railway reached the town in 1850, the incoming mail coaches ceased to operate. Mail coaches still had to be used to carry mail westwards from Swansea, but as the railway extended further, so the mail coaches were taken out of service.

The year 1850 was significant for the postal service in Swansea, as this was when the railway first brought the mail to the town. The introduction of the Penny Post had greatly increased the amount of mail being sent and, as a consequence, it became necessary to provide new accommodation for the town's principal post office. A new office was provided for the post office at 12 Fisher Street, which opened on 20 June 1849. Complaints were legion about the unsuitability of these premises; they were cramped, inconveniently placed in a minor street and difficult to adapt to Post Office business.

The Fisher Street premises were only ever considered to be temporary accommodation. Plans were soon under way for the building of a new post office for the town. The architect chosen was Mr Bayliss, and the site was adjacent to the castle in Castle Bailey Street. Mr Bayliss favoured a Tudor Gothic style, and work began in 1856. Two years later, the building was ready for occupation, and opened officially on 1 April 1858. However, by 1860, less than two years later, there were complaints that the new office was too small, overcrowded and needed replacing. To ease the situation there, a branch office (BO) was opened in Adelaide Street in 1867. This was the Docks BO, which stayed in Adelaide Street until 1870, when it then moved to Coleridge House at the bottom of Wind Street. It was joined in this building by the telegraph office when all telegraph services were concentrated in the hands of the Post Office. In 1883, parcel post was concentrated there, too.

In 1878, it was suggested that a new head post office should be built in Wind Street, but it was twenty years before any actual action was taken towards this aim. Work started in the summer of 1898, and on 15 December 1901 the new head office was opened. There were still a few finishing touches to attend to, but Swansea now had a large, dignified head post office, which was to remain in use for a century.

Two sub-offices had opened in the town in 1848, one in Orange Street, the other in High Street. They only lasted until 1858, when they were replaced by pillar boxes. The next sub-office was the previously mentioned Docks BO in

New Head Post Office, Castle Bailey Street. Print by Bayliss, the architect.

1867, but from 1870 to the end of the century, sub-post offices were opened at a regular rate throughout the area for which the Swansea head post office was responsible. As well as the town, this stretched over the Gower Peninsula, the Swansea Valley up to Abercrave and the Lliw Valley area. For a time, a number of Carmarthenshire offices also came under its control.

The huge expansion of postal services from 1840 was catered for, with the head office building in Wind Street being expanded in 1916, and again in 1924 and 1967. In the heart of the city, a new Crown post office was opened in the Kingsway, which also housed the local Philatelic Counter, and in High Street next to the Swansea Dock Workers Hall and Institute. Both of these, along with the head post office in Wind Street, have closed. There is now just one post office in the centre of Swansea, on the first floor of the W.H. Smith shop in the Quadrant shopping centre.

13

ENTERTAINMENT

THEATRES AND CINEMAS

From the middle of the seventeenth century, travelling theatre companies would hire the Town Hall as a venue for theatrical performances, such as plays and musical events. As I have already noted, by the late eighteenth century, the Town Hall was no longer adequate for these shows and the bold step was taken to open a purpose-built theatre in Anchor Court, just off Wind Street. It enjoyed considerable success, and the decision was made to build larger and more up-to-date premises.

The Theatre Royal opened in 1807 on a site at the corner of Temple Street and Goat Street. Today, the clothing chain Zara has a store on the same site. Despite attracting renowned actors to perform there, the Theatre Royal only enjoyed sporadic success. In 1864, the Music Hall opened in Cradock Street, bringing additional competition for the Theatre Royal. Consequently, it closed in 1898 and was demolished, making way for the David Evans department store.

The Music Hall became the Albert Hall in 1881, functioning more as a concert hall than a theatre. Oscar Wilde performed there, as did Dame Adelina Patti. In 1901, it was the venue for the town's memorial concert for Queen Victoria. Another sombre memorial event was held in

1912, when Swansea remembered the victims of the sinking of the *Titanic*.

The old building was given a new lease of life with the arrival of moving pictures. In the 1920s, a new projection box was installed along with sound equipment. For the next fifty years it was Swansea's leading cinema. In 1977 it closed and was taken over by the Rank Organisation and suffered the same fate as so many cinemas up and down the country – it was turned into a bingo hall. Mecca took over a few years later, but by 2007 it had closed, and today, though still standing, it is boarded up and gradually deteriorating.

Down in Wind Street, in the meantime, the Star Inn had been demolished late in the 1850s and was replaced by a large wooden amphitheatre with the rather grand name, The Prince of Wales Amphitheatre. This was a name that it evidently had difficulty living up to. It was often referred to as the 'Swansea Circus', which might have been its official name for a time.

The building hosted a wide variety of different entertainments and, on one celebrated occasion in 1872, allowed a female impersonator to perform. His name was Ernest Boulton, and the *Cambrian* newspaper demanded that the establishment be closed as it considered such performances to be a threat to public morals.

The Melville family took over the establishment over in 1874 and renamed it the Star Theatre in 1875. It became the most popular theatre, providing musical acts, comedies, tragedies and melodramas. After twenty years of success, however, the Melvilles suffered some bad luck. In 1895, two of the family died within a couple of months of each other, and the theatre was put up for sale.

William Coutts, who already had theatre interests elsewhere in the country, purchased the premises and continued to provide the successful and popular mix of entertainment of the Melville days. In fact, Coutts was making enough money that, in 1905, he could purchase the Palace Theatre in High Street. The Star continued to offer live theatre until 1915, when it closed briefly and then reopened as a cinema called the Royal Theatre. In the 1920s, it reverted to live theatre again. But, the biggest change was to come. Talking pictures forced a dramatic change on the Star, as it was rebuilt in 1931 and became the Rialto Cinema. As such, it survived up to the 1960s, when it closed and in 1968 was demolished and the site redeveloped.

Swansea had, although not at the same time, two Empire Theatres. The earliest began life in 1888 as the Pavilion Music Hall & Theatre of Varieties, and occupied a triangular site near High Street Station. Oswald Stoll took over the Pavilion and renamed it the Empire Palace, which was shortened by everyone to the Empire. Many big names in the entertainment world, such as Marie Lloyd, George Robey and Dan Leno, were attracted to the Empire. However, Oswald Stoll opened a new theatre in Oxford Street in 1900 and took the name Empire with him. This new theatre was much larger, more modern and elegant. All the big names that came to Swansea now preferred to perform at the Oxford Street Empire.

Up in High Street, the Empire there changed owners and changed its name to the Palace Theatre of Varieties. But, with three theatres in town, competition was tough. The Oxford Street Empire took the top names, whilst the Star in Wind Street had smaller touring companies and the popular melodramas. The Palace had to make do with what was left. Things were looking bleak when, in 1905, bolstered with the profits from the Star, William Coutts bought the Palace and was able to book attractions at both theatres that did not compete with each other.

However, movies were the new craze and, in 1912, Coutts allowed the Palace to become a cinema, calling it the Palace Bioscope and then the Popular Picture Palace. With purpose-built cinemas drawing the audience away from the Palace, Coutts went back to live performances. In 1932, though, the Palace was wired for cinema sound. It worked on as a cinema until 1949, when a fire in the building caused sufficient damage that the building was unused for four years, until in 1953 it briefly became a repertory theatre. Facing closure again in 1955, it was rescued by the Swansea Little Theatre, who used it as their base, staying for six years. During this period, the Little Theatre put on a performance of a play called *Have a Cigarette*, which was the first professional stage appearance for a certain Anthony Hopkins.

The owners of the building decided to close it in 1961 and make way for offices, and when this did not happen, the building reopened in 1967 as a bingo hall. It then spent a short time as a furniture warehouse, and then as a nightclub. Finally closing in 1992, the building is now empty and neglected. In September 2019, a fire broke out on the roof of the building and rumour has it that the City Council will soon buy it and undertake a thorough renovation. It is one of Swansea's iconic buildings, with a long and interesting history, so perhaps good fortune will smile on the Palace once more.

The Empire Theatre in Oxford Street attracted, as I have said, all the top names. In 1910, both Stan Laurel and Charlie Chaplin appeared on the same bill. Stan Laurel was part of a Fred Karno touring comedy, whilst Charlie Chaplin was top of the bill. On one occasion, Lily Langtry, the 'Jersey Lily' and intimate of King Edward VII, appeared in a play called *The Frenchwoman*. Comedians galore came to the Empire, including Tommy Trinder, Max Miller, Max

Wall and Ted Ray. And, of course, in 1952 Stan Laurel returned, this time with Oliver Hardy to perform there.

A talent show for young performers was held at the Empire early in 1940 and attracted hopefuls from all over the country. Amongst them were two young men who met and became friends, launching a partnership that was to endure for many years. These were Eric Morecambe and Ernie Wise, who came back in 1948, still relatively unknown, to perform in the pantomime of that year. The days of the Empire were numbered, however, as the popularity of TV drew audiences away. Pantomime was still popular, but at other times of the year, audiences slumped. In 1957, therefore, the Empire closed and was demolished, allowing retail development in its place.

The Grand Theatre opened its doors in 1897, the opening ceremony being carried out by Dame Adelina Patti, the famous opera singer, who lived at Craig-y-Nos in the Swansea Valley. Top actors, such as Sir Henry Irving, graced the Grand with their performances, along with organisations like the Welsh National Opera. The support of Swansea City Council, who now own the theatre, ensured its survival, expansion and commercial viability. It continues to provide top-class entertainment for Swansea's citizens.

Cinema, though, was the upcoming entertainment phenomenon. As has been seen, some of Swansea's theatres took on a cine-variety role to boost audiences, whilst others gave up on live theatre and remodelled themselves as cinemas.

The first purpose-built cinema in Swansea was the Castle Cinema, which opened in 1913. Situated at the end of Worcester Place, next to the site of Swansea Castle, it enjoyed a long period of relative success until 1967, when it was refurbished. However, in order to continue in business, it turned to soft-porn films. It finally closed as a cinema in 1991, and became Laserzone, which still exists today.

In 1914, the Carlton Cinema de Luxe opened on Oxford Street, next door to the Empire Theatre. It had an imposing façade, which subsequently was given Grade II listed building status. It also boasted a first-floor café, which was accessed by a grand staircase, and during the 1920s was popular with townsfolk. It was closed in October 1977 and whilst the façade was saved, the remainder was demolished and a Waterstones bookshop opened there.

The Elysium Theatre also opened in 1914 on High Street. This cinema was a two-floor venue which also had a small stage so that some variety or music-hall acts could perform there. The building was shared with the Swansea Dock Worker's Hall and Working Men's Club. In 1960, the cinema was converted into a bingo hall. Parts of the building continued in use as Labour Party offices, but in 1994 the whole was closed and boarded up. The building still stands but is in an extremely poor state.

Another purpose-built cinema was the Plaza, on what is now the Kingsway. Opened in 1931, it was at that time the largest cinema in Wales. Designed by a Cardiff architect, Howard Williams, it brought the glitzy world of Hollywood to Swansea. It boasted a massive organ, sumptuous surroundings in the foyer, wood panels carved with Celtic and Welsh motifs and, after 1953, CinemaScope and stereophonic sound. It was a true picture palace.

However, its magnificence did not save it as, in 1965, it was demolished and replaced by the modern Odeon cinema, which actually had a Tesco supermarket on the ground floor. In 1997, the Odeon closed and the building was converted into the Oceana nightclub. That, too, closed and was demolished in 2017, but at the time of writing we only know that the site is to become a 'Digital Village'.

One feature of cinema, and something which showed how popular a form of entertainment it was, is the fact that cinemas opened in the suburbs as well as the centre of town. Uplands, Manselton, Townhill, Sketty, St Thomas, Gowerton, Pontardulais, Landore, Clydach-on-Tawe, Fforestfach, Mumbles and Morriston all had their own cinemas and, in some cases, two.

SPORT

I have already mentioned the arrival of cricket at St Helen's, and indeed, many memorable games between Glamorgan and a variety of visiting teams have taken place here. The St Helen's ground hosted not only cricket, but rugby, too. In 1882, the first international rugby match played in Wales took place at St Helen's when an English team played Wales there. The last international rugby match to be played in Swansea was also played at St Helen's on 22 March 1952 when Wales played France, winning 9–5. The All-Whites, the Swansea rugby club team, continued to play against visiting national sides including, memorably, the 1953 visit of the New Zealand All Blacks, whom Swansea held to a 6–6 draw.

Association Football was being played in Swansea amongst local village sides during the latter part of the nineteenth century, but it was not until 1912 that a professional Swansea team came into existence. They were immediately dubbed 'the Swans', and it was 1920 before they joined the English league structure. This had been going since 1888, so Swansea were, indeed, latecomers in that respect.

They were able to play their games at the Vetch Field in the Sandfields area of the town and drew huge crowds of spectators for their fixtures. A rough financial patch followed in the 1980s, despite have joined the First Division of the English League in 1982. However, a local businessman called Doug Sharpe saved the day, and the club was revived and carried on. It moved on to a new stadium at Morfa – the Liberty Stadium – and enjoyed several successful seasons in the English Premier League. The Vetch Field was destined for redevelopment once the football club moved out, but it has, instead, become a community resource with open spaces and allotments.

Today, Swansea boasts the National Pool adjacent to the University Playing Fields at Ashleigh Road, and leisure centres have been incorporated into many of the city's secondary schools, so providing sporting opportunities for many. The Swansea Harriers are a world-renowned athletics club, who can boast many champions at all levels.

COX'S FARM

It may seem a little macabre to include the story of Swansea Gaol under the heading 'Entertainment', but in the nineteenth century executions drew huge crowds from far and wide. In medieval times, executions would probably have been carried out in the castle and, from Tudor times, on Gibbet Hill at Dyfatty. It was customary for corpses of executed felons to hang on the gibbet for months afterwards. In 1901 the name of the hill was changed to North Hill.

Executions, wherever they were held, were a form of public entertainment, and were sometimes referred to as a 'Roman Holiday'. Swansea Gaol was built in 1825 as a House of Correction, rather than a fully blown prison for convicted prisoners. The first public execution to take place there was on 20 March 1858, when two Greek sailors, Zelephanta and Aleppi, were hanged on the top of the gaol wall for the murder of a shipmate, named Mitropanis, at the North Dock. It is noteworthy that the two men were arrested, tried, condemned and executed all within thirty-three days.

The last public hanging to be carried out at the gaol was of Robert Coe in April 1866. After that, hangings were carried out within the prison walls, although crowds did often gather outside to hear word that the deed had been done. The last man to be hanged at Swansea Gaol was Vivian Teed, who was convicted of the murder of William Williams, the postmaster at Fforestfach post office. Teed, who was unemployed and 24 years old at the time of the murder, had taken a hammer from his father's tool box and used it to beat the 73-year-old postmaster to death. Whilst Teed confessed to the murder, he claimed that demons in his head had made him act as he did. The question, therefore, when he came to trial was whether he was suffering diminished responsibility. The jury took three attempts, but did find him guilty. He also lost his appeal and petitions for mercy were ignored. There was no dramatic last-minute reprieve from the Home Secretary. On 6 May 1958, Teed was hanged, and became a tiny postscript to history.

Why 'Cox's Farm'? The first two governors of the prison were named William Cox – father and son. The name just stuck in popular parlance.

14

THE GREAT WAR

'It'll all be over by Christmas' was a phrase on many people's lips when war was declared against Germany and Austria–Hungary on 4 August 1914. So, the announcement by the Board of Agriculture in London on 7 August that the country had wheat stocks to last four months would not have caused undue alarm. However, food prices did rise in the early days of the war, due to increased demand as a result of hoarding, and the temptation to make a few extra pennies on the part of some shopkeepers. The Board of Trade introduced 'official food prices' on 14 August in an attempt to put a halt to these practices.

RECRUITMENT

The supply of food was to be a constant worry for the authorities throughout the war. However, for the military authorities it was the supply of men that was their main concern. Lord Kitchener, who was a hero in most Britons' eyes after his exploits at Khartoum, was made Secretary of State for War, and he anticipated that, rather than having ended by Christmas, the war would go on far longer. His aim was to recruit 100,000 men aged between 21 and 30.

All over the country, men rushed to join the colours, with Swansea having a similar reaction. By December, over 800,000 men had joined up, but there will still very many, who for a number of reasons, did not volunteer. Some 8,000 men in Swansea had either returned to the forces or joined as volunteers. In September 1914, it was decided to form a Swansea Battalion that would comprise volunteers from the town, and would be attached to the Welsh Regiment. In December 1914, the battalion left for Rhyl and a period of training. Christmas was getting perilously close, and there was no sign of the war being over.

Throughout 1915, recruitment campaigns were held all over Swansea, with meetings being held in halls, schools and some even in the open air. Still, nationally, not enough men were volunteering, and in January 1916 the Military Service Act came into force, bringing with it conscription. There were exemptions, and many men were able to avoid the call-up because their work or commitments were of national importance. Many, though, tried to hoodwink the authorities, which rarely worked, and they ended up being transferred into the military anyway.

One category that particularly riled the authorities were the conscientious objectors. There were many 'c.o.'s' who firmly believed they were right not to fight, but did other service in the armed forces. Conscientious objectors were only exempted from combatant roles, so they were still expected to work as ambulance men, stretcher bearers, etc. Some conscientious objectors refused those duties too and were either imprisoned or court-martialled as a result. Some Swansea conscientious objectors were imprisoned, such as Harold Beynon, who spent time in Wormwood Scrubs and Dartmoor.

CONTROLLED PORT STATUS

Swansea was a controlled port, and much of the town and outlying districts were prohibited areas, where a range of activities were forbidden. These even included sketching.

Belgian refugees had arrived in large numbers over the first months of the war, and had been welcomed by the townspeople. The authorities in London, however, realised that a large concentration of alien refugees in any one town was not such a good idea, and they made controlled ports no longer available for refugee resettlement. Its status as a controlled port meant that from January 1915 groups of alien refugees would no longer be sent there to be resettled.

THE ROLE OF WOMEN

With thousands of local men away at the front, it was the women of Swansea who stepped into their shoes. Women took over roles as tram and bus conductresses, postwomen and, of course, working in the munitions factories. Landore had the main Swansea munitions factory, and with more and more men volunteering for the forces it became necessary to employ women to work there. They became known as the 'munitionettes', and they even had their own football team!

Errand boys, who would have been too young to enlist, found themselves being transferred to the work that older men would traditionally have done, and some even ended up in munitions work. Their jobs as errand boys were then taken up by errand girls. In an age when telephones were few and far between, many offices relied on errand boys to take messages, documents and other items about the town, so there were plenty of opportunities for girls to step into this work.

One unusual development that came about as a result of the war was the appearance of 'lady patrols' on the streets of Swansea (some other towns had them too). The aim of these patrols was to act as extra eyes and ears for the police. They were not concerned with prostitutes, but more with what were described as 'giddy young girls', who were, it seems, a bit like the fans of pop groups in the 1960s. They pursued soldiers who were home on leave or based in the town with a sort of doe-eyed infatuation. There had been cases of soldiers not being able to walk along the street because of the attention of these girls. By July 1917, there were eighteen ladies' patrols operating in Swansea, so it is likely that they had the desired effect in deterring these girls from pursuing soldiers. However, I don't think the soldiers were asked their opinion about being spared the attentions of these pesky lasses – public morals were at stake, after all!

One traditional role for women was that of nurse. Nurses were certainly in demand in Swansea, for there were hospitals set aside for wounded soldiers. The Red Cross were the first, in August 1914, to get themselves prepared for the inevitable influx of wounded. They used the Llewellyn Hall at the YMCA and Sketty Church Hall as hospitals, fitting them out with donated items as well as items from their own stores. The first of these to be used was Sketty Church Hall in November, when a group of twelve men arrived who had been wounded at the Battle of the Aisne. The following month saw the YMCA receive its first wounded and, in May 1915, a large private house called 'Heddfan' received patients.

Larger premises were needed and, in answer to the call, Miss Dulcie Vivian allowed her house called 'Parc Wern' to be used; generously, she met the cost of converting it. Similarly, Mr Cory Yeo allowed his house at Danycoed in

West Cross to be used, and he met the cost of conversion. In 1917, the new building of the Infants' School in Brynmill was adapted as a hospital.

SPANISH FLU

With the war drawing to a close and the Allies at last pushing the Germans back, another crisis came along to cause more misery and death. The Spanish Flu epidemic began, it is thought, in March 1918 at a US Army camp in the United States and was carried across to Europe from there. It was a particularly virulent variant of the H1N1 virus, and got the name 'Spanish Flu' because Spain, as a neutral country, did not have censorship and so outbreaks in that country could be freely reported in the press there.

As the epidemic turned into a pandemic, the problem facing the authorities became clear. In Swansea, cases of those falling victim to the disease increased from July 1918 onward. Between May and December, sixty-one deaths were recorded in the under-20 age group, and there were seventy-four deaths in those over 41. However, it was in the 20–41-year-old age group that the most deaths were recorded – 121. Clearly, fit, young people were most at risk. Official advice included sleeping in a well-ventilated room, avoiding crowded places, washing hands and keeping clothing and bedding away from that of healthy people.

The pandemic killed up to 100 million people worldwide, with the Welsh total at around 11,000. Swansea lost 434 and it is known that its death rate was lower than Cardiff and Newport, but why is not clear. By comparison, the number of men from Swansea killed in the war is estimated at about 3,000.

15

THE GUILDHALL

The first town hall in Swansea had been built in 1585 close against the walls of Swansea Castle, on the site that was later used for the new post office in 1852. When this became too small, a new Guildhall was built in Somerset Place in 1825, with extra accommodation being added between 1848 and 1852. This building remained in use until new accommodation could be provided. The building continued in use, being part of Dynevor School for a while, and it is now the Dylan Thomas Centre, a venue for arts projects and the like.

The period between the two world wars was one of acute economic depression, with high unemployment and attendant hardship. To help alleviate this in the Swansea area, the County Council undertook a number of capital projects. The most noticeable was the building of a new administrative headquarters on a site in Victoria Park.

The Guildhall, which includes the Brangwyn Hall, was designed by Sir Percy Thomas, a Cardiff architect. He created Swansea's first building in the Modern Movement style, with hardly any external decoration, which has been compared to the building erected by Mussolini's regime in Italy at the same time. It was a nod to classical styling, but with less ornament. The interior, however, enjoys much more in the way of decoration, but again with a nod to the classical. The building was opened by the Duke of Kent on 23 October 1934.

In addition, the council undertook the building of Tir John North Power Station, which began operating in 1935; the Cefn Coed Mental Hospital, which opened in 1932 and the Main Drainage Scheme of 1936. By using labour under the unemployment relief schemes initiated by the government, much of the cost of these projects was reduced.

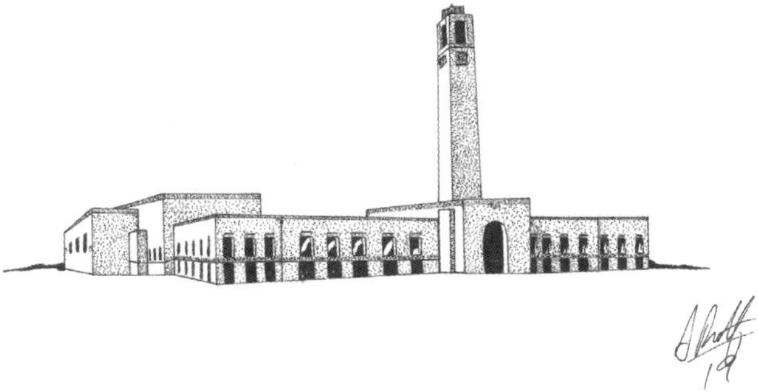

The Guildhall was built in 1934 in Victoria Park. It includes the famed Brangwyn panels, originally intended for the House of Lords. They now adorn Brangwyn Hall.

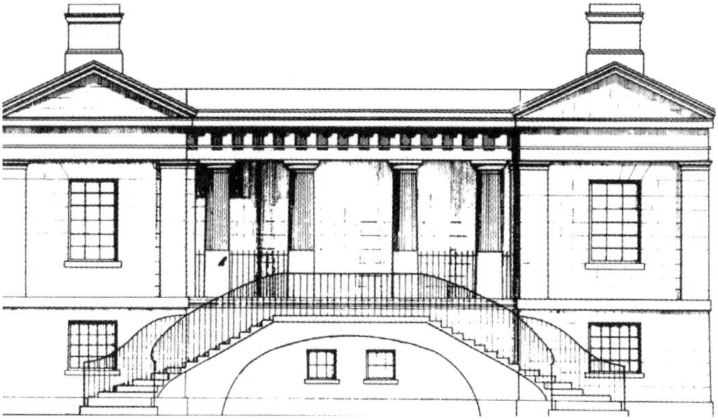

Architect's drawing of the new Guildhall built on the Burrows in 1829.

16

THE SECOND WORLD WAR

Despite the lessons learnt during the Great War regarding the need for anti-aircraft defences and the need for a civilian force of volunteers to act as a back-up to the regular forces should there be an invasion, not very much was done during the inter-war period towards the necessary preparations. As the 1930s progressed, though, and the threat from Germany became more obvious, things began to take shape.

It was thought by those in command that Swansea and the other South Wales ports were too far distant from the Luftwaffe airbases in Germany for there to be a risk of bombing. However, the rapid occupation of Norway, northern France and the Low Countries brought the Welsh ports well within range as targets. While Portsmouth, a town of similar size and importance to Swansea, had been provided with forty-four heavy anti-aircraft guns, Swansea had only three. Barrage balloons, which gave protection by preventing low flying and so made bombing less accurate, were another problem. London had something in the region of 300 of these by the summer of 1940; in South Wales sixteen balloons had to cover the entire area.

A few tentative bombing raids in June 1940 soon brought action, however. The first to be hit was Danygraig Road, where luckily there was little damage and no casualties. New anti-aircraft sites were established at Winch Wen, on

Mumbles Hill, at Ravenhill and Townhill. Light anti-aircraft emplacements appeared around the docks, at Ashleigh Road and at Blackpill. Mobile guns on mountings were placed at Penllergaer, from where they could be brought into the town at short notice. A searchlight battery was set up at St Helen's Cricket Ground. Mostly, these installations were manned by members of the Swansea Home Guard.

With the fall of France in June 1940, Britain was in the grip of invasion fever. It was feared that the Germans, now camped just across Channel in northern France, would invade a weakened and demoralised Britain. At coastal sites that were thought to be particularly vulnerable to seaborne landings, a host of different measures were taken to try to protect the areas. Concrete pillboxes and other emplacements were built (some of these still exist in Gower), barbed-wire entanglements, tank traps and roadblocks were set up.

The Secretary of State for War, Anthony Eden, had begun in May to create an organisation called the Local Defence Volunteers. Drawn from men aged between 17 and 65 who were not, for various reasons, in military service, this was an organisation with the main object of patrolling and guarding factories, railways and other vital locations. They also manned anti-aircraft guns, searchlights, barrage balloons and other defensive measures. The portrayal of these men in *Dad's Army,* it seems, was quite accurate. Brave men who, for various reasons including age or infirmity, were unable to join regular forces, but were nevertheless quite willing to lay down their lives in defence of their country.

The Air Raid Precautions, Home Guard, Police and emergency services were well organised in Swansea and, as a result, the loss of life in the town during the Blitz was much less than it might have been. Sporadic bombing raids throughout the months of June to October 1940 did little damage and caused few casualties. The worst raid was on the night of 10–11 August. It lasted one hour, and there was damage to houses in Cwmbwrla, Manselton and Brynhyfryd. The main GWR line was cut in two places. In Penfilia Road, an air-raid shelter took a direct hit and its five occupants were all killed.

THE THREE NIGHTS' BLITZ

November and December of 1940 were quiet months for Swansea, with no air raids, but on 17 January 1941 the town suffered its heaviest raid, with fifty-five people killed and extensive damage recorded. Things went quiet then for another four weeks, and then we come to 19 February 1941 and the first night of the Three Nights' Blitz.

As a result of this onslaught, High Street, Temple Street, Castle Street, Caer Street, Goat Street, Calvert Street, College Street, Gower Street, Park Street, Oxford Street and Waterloo Street all suffered heavy damage; some were so devastated that they effectively disappeared from the map. The market was gutted by fire, Swansea Victoria Station had its glass roof destroyed and 7,000 people were effectively homeless. Over 800 high-explosive bombs were dropped over the three nights along with some 11,000 incendiary devices. It was a devastating blow to the town, although the docks and Lower Swansea Valley experienced virtually no damage at all.

Among the well-known buildings lost in the Three Nights' Blitz was the Ben Evans department store. This was the pinnacle of luxury shopping in Swansea, situated in Castle Bailey Street. Often referred to as 'the Harrods of Wales', it was opened in 1898 on the site of Plas House, a sixteenth-century gentleman's residence that had declined over the centuries and was finally demolished in 1840.

An 1826 print by Stockdale of the west front of the Plas Manor House.

Opposite Ben Evans, on the other side of Temple Street, was David Evans, another department store, built at about the same time, on the site of the Theatre Royal. This, too, was destroyed in the Three Nights' Blitz. Unlike Ben Evans, though, David Evans was rebuilt after the war, and remained a feature of Swansea's shopping centre for another forty years. The Ben Evans site was cleared and became Castle Gardens.

There were further air raids on Swansea over the next two years, mostly in 1941. There was just one raid in 1942, when a large number of incendiary bombs were dropped around Birchgrove. Luckily, damage was negligible and no one was hurt. The last raid, almost exactly two years after the Three Nights' Blitz, occurred on 16 February 1943. As well as high-explosive bombs, this raid included phosphorous bombs and incendiary devices. The bulk of the bombs were dropped on the town centre and along Neath Road, Hafod, St Thomas and across town in Brynmill. Thirty-four people died as a result of this raid.

Visiting Dignitaries

The severity of the Three Nights' Blitz brought a number of high-profile visitors to Swansea, the most important being King George VI and Queen Elizabeth, who came to see the devastation on 19 March 1941. Prime Minister Winston Churchill visited the town on 11 April, followed by the Home Secretary, Mr Herbert Morrison, on 23 August. The Prime Minister of Australia, the Rt Hon. R.G. Menzies, came to inspect the damage on 30 April and, during the visit, inspected the Swansea Home Guard. This was the second time in a week on parade for an inspection, as the Home Secretary had done the same just seven days earlier – and a cold, wet day that had been!

RAF FAIRWOOD COMMON

Out in Gower, an RAF station was constructed on Fairwood Common, and it became the home of 125 'Newfoundland' Squadron. They received a high-ranking visitor in October 1942, when Newfoundland's Commissioner for Justice and Defence, the Hon. H.E. Emerson, arrived to congratulate the men of the squadron. The following year, another top-ranking visitor was Air Marshal HRH the Duke of Gloucester, who went to tour the base.

Over the three years that RAF Fairwood Common was an operational station, Polish, Czech, Canadian and Australian squadrons were stationed there, in addition to thirty-two British squadrons or detachments. After D-Day in 1944, the status of the station changed, but it still hosted French, Norwegian and Dutch squadrons, plus more Polish, Canadian and Australian units.

After the war, RAF Fairwood Common became redundant as an RAF base and was turned into a civilian airport. It was never really anything more than a small airport from which tiny aircraft took pleasure flights over the Gower Peninsula and the Severn Estuary. Attempts have been made to establish scheduled flights to other parts of the UK and to Ireland, but none were successful.

AMERICAN TROOPS IN SWANSEA

In the months before D-Day, American troops were stationed throughout southern Britain, conveniently placed for disembarkation ports. British and Canadian troops, similarly preparing for the 'off', were based near south-eastern ports, whereas the American troops tended to be based near the south-western ports. The US V Corps (2 Division) was centred on Swansea. Camps were established in Singleton Park, Ashleigh Road, Oystermouth, Scurlage in South Gower, Penclawdd in North Gower, Penllergaer, Morriston and at Briton Ferry.

Maintaining a high level of morale amongst the troops was helped by the efforts of local people who provided entertainment, such as dances and concerts. My own mother, who was in her twenties during the war and was a keen attender of social dances, said how much better things were when the American soldiers were in Gower. Life became one long social whirl, with the generous Americans treating the locals as a way of thanking them for their welcome.

One little anecdote that has come down to us from this time concerns the Adelphi Hotel in Wind Street, which was popular with American troops. One of these was a young chap by the name of Rocco Marciano. Being well aware of the need to keep his body in tip-top shape, he would normally have a glass of milk when out with his buddies. This particular night was just the same, and 'Rocky' ordered his glass of milk. He was overheard by an Australian sergeant, who then taunted Rocky about his choice of beverage. Maybe the Australian was soon regretting his decision!

Come D-Day, though, and the atmosphere changed. The 2nd Division was a follow-up to the Assault Corps that had led the way, and they disembarked from Swansea Docks to land on Omaha Beach on 7 and 8 June 1944. They left behind them fond memories!

AT THE END OF THE WAR

VE (Victory in Europe) Day and VJ (Victory over Japan) Day brought the people of Swansea out on the streets in celebration. Street parties were held, soldiers who were home on leave were feted and everyone breathed a united sigh of relief. However, the town was in ruins, and husbands and sons were still in Europe, where a shattered Germany had to be rebuilt.

Swansea also had to be rebuilt. Indeed, the nation had to be rebuilt, and the government was well aware that there needed to be some order and planning in this process. Being a Labour Government, it wanted there to be a greater element of central control over the reconstruction of the country and, in 1947, it passed the Town & Country Planning Act. Local authorities were required to develop a plan for reconstruction and development, and it included the requirement that all new buildings had to have planning permission.

In Swansea, once the corporation had acquired the freehold of the devastated centre of the town, its plan, which had been prepared in 1946, could go ahead.

17

PEACETIME PROGRESS

RECONSTRUCTION OF THE TOWN CENTRE

The plan from 1946 included major changes to the road layout in Swansea town centre. The narrow streets of the past were replaced with broad boulevards and traffic flow was improved with the introduction of roundabouts and dual carriageways. The main shopping street was intended to be the Kingsway, running west to east from St Helen's Road to the new Kingsway roundabout, from which radiated Princess Way, heading towards St Mary's Church; College Street, joining up with High Street and Castle Street and Orchard Street, which headed towards Alexandra Road and High Street Station. In creating the Kingsway, both Gower Street and Northampton Place disappeared.

In addition to the Kingsway, shopping was intended to be concentrated on High Street and Castle Street. Creating the Castle Gardens on the site of Ben Evans' department store was one effort made to shift shopping away from that part of town. However, the corporation, who seemed to dither over every decision, then allowed Sidney Heath to build his Tudoresque department store on Caer Street, which runs along the southern edge of Castle Gardens. They also dithered for eighteen months over where to put the new

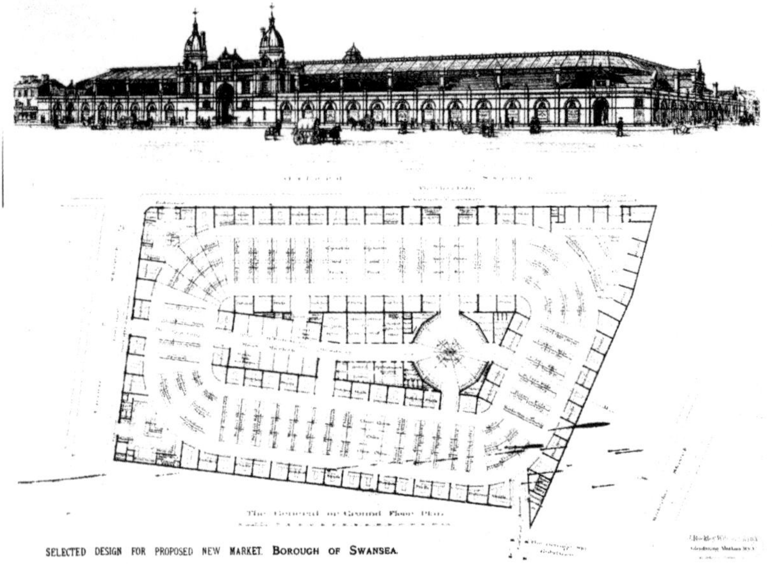

Architect's drawing of the proposed new market in Oxford Street, 1895.

market. After the destruction of the old market, stalls had been set up on a temporary basis inside its walls, so it was no surprise that the decision was made to leave the market where it was. The stalls were moved to the Wassail Square area, and a new market – one of the best in Wales, if not the whole country – was built on the site.

There was much criticism of the corporation's lack of urgency in getting the redevelopment moving. Plymouth, which had suffered similarly and provided a good comparison, had made great leaps in providing new shops and roads, car parks and places of entertainment in their town centre. Swansea moved but slowly, and whilst a few people felt that it was good not to rush and make mistakes, the majority wanted life to get back to normal in a vibrant town centre. The Kingsway was the first part of the plan to be finished and when, in November 1950, Princess Margaret came to perform the official opening, it did restore some optimism amongst Swansea folk.

As the market was always a draw for Swansea folk, allowing it to remain on Oxford Street meant that people would naturally head in that direction, giving it the edge over the Kingsway as a shopping street. The modern boulevard approach in creating the Kingsway ultimately worked against it as a draw for shoppers. It seemed like an awfully long way to 'nip' across to a shop and, whilst some shops thrived there – I personally remember John Hall (Tools) Ltd because they stocked model railway items amongst the toys on the first floor – the street gradually became the home for a number of banks and building societies.

This was eventually recognised when the site of the temporary market in Wassail Square become the preferred choice for the Quadrant Shopping Centre, taking the shopping focus even further away from the Kingsway and High Street, both of which have suffered decline in recent years. The attempt to take shopping even further towards Oystermouth Road did not meet with success, as the St David's Shopping Centre did not catch on and has largely been demolished in favour of car-parking space.

However, returning to the early 1950s, High Street was then seen as an attractive prospect for businesses coming into Swansea. In November 1951, at long last, some might say, new shops were occupied by W.H. Smith, and next door, Eynon's, a café and bakers. In 1952, Hepworth's, the gentleman's outfitters, and Stead & Simpson, footwear retailers, also opened on High Street. In the meantime, C&A, a store selling men's and women's fashions, opened in Portland Street, on a corner shared with the Kingsway. Later in the year, Boots, the Chemist opened a shop on the corner of Oxford Street and Princess Way, opposite Castle Gardens. For many years, this was known as 'Boots Corner'.

Marks & Spencer had been in Swansea since it had opened a store in Goat Street Arcade in 1919. After several moves into temporary accommodation during the intervening years – it never left Swansea – it opened a brand new store on Oxford Street on 23 April 1953. It boasted a large ground-floor shopping experience, and there was general relief that the firm was open for business again.

Back on the Kingsway, the gentlemen's outfitters and school uniform suppliers, Wildings opened their Swansea store in that same year. In 1954 Swansea saw the reopening of the David Evans department store, pretty much on the same site that it had occupied before the war. In 1956, the Co-op opened a store with two floors and a basement opposite Marks & Spencer. The following year saw a branch of British Home Stores open next door to Marks & Spencer, making a superb shopping destination at the eastern end of Oxford Street.

Swansea was certainly getting back to business, and although the new shops tended to be branches of national chains, there were still independent local shops scattered amongst them. Then in 1959 came the icing on the cake. St Mary's Church had been restored according to the original plans that had been prepared and used to carry out its 1895 restoration. Now that the work was complete, Queen Elizabeth, the Queen Mother came to Swansea to attend the re-consecration service at the church. More than anything else, this visit spoke to the populace that the war and its aftermath were now consigned to history.

Swansea could look forward to a brighter and more prosperous future. It was time to say 'hello' to the 1960s.

THE 1960S

Three important changes occurred during the 1960s. Firstly, coal mining within the boundaries of Swansea ceased when the Felin Fran Mine closed in 1965. An industry that had existed in Swansea since medieval times had gone. Other industries were clinging on, such as tinplate, copper ingots and steel, and continued through the decade, but their end was in sight.

Then, Singleton Hospital was built on a part of Singleton Park in the mid-1960s. There had been agitation for greater hospital provision in Swansea for several decades and now here was a modern, fully equipped hospital. Morriston Hospital had grown up piecemeal and had to wait another twenty years before its refurbishment could begin.

The third change was the opening of the Driver & Vehicle Licensing Centre (DVLC) in 1965. This was part of government initiatives to move civil service jobs away from London and the south-east of England. The site for the new building overlooks the M4 motorway just west of Morriston and close by Morriston Crematorium. At sixteen storeys high, the building still dominates the skyline here, and can be seen for several miles when viewed from the north and west. Its workforce of 4,000 at that time made it the largest single employer in Swansea other than the local authority. It had a knock-on effect on the Royal Mail, who now had to provide extra facilities – leading to extra jobs – to deal with the increased amount of mail generated as a result.

The fourth major change was in 1969, when Swansea was granted city status as part of the celebrations marking the investiture of the Prince of Wales at Caernarfon Castle.

THE 1970S

Three major decisions helped change the face of Swansea in the 1970s. Firstly, the North Dock, which had closed in 1928, was completely filled in and became the site of Plantasia, a cinema, ten-pin bowling alley and some retail outlets. There was also a large car park provided for the customers of these establishments.

A further redevelopment has taken place recently in 2017, whereby the Plantasia building, cinema and ten-pin bowling alley remain, but an improved range of retail outlets have replaced the earlier ones, and a new drive-through coffee shop has been built. Car parking, however, has remained available there. The northern part of the old dock site was developed for retail use in the 1980s, and no further work has taken place there. One of the former tenants, Homebase, a DIY superstore, closed in 2018, and its premises have been redeveloped by Lidl to create a large supermarket.

The second change was to the organisation of local government. In 1974 Swansea ceased to be a county borough, and became a district council within the newly formed West Glamorgan County Council. Four districts made up the new county – Swansea, Neath, Port Talbot and the newly created Lliw Valley which covered Gorseinon, Pontardulais and the top of the Swansea Valley. Swansea, however, was able to keep its status as a city, and also gained the Gower Peninsula with the abolition of the Gower Rural District Council.

The most obvious change for the people living in Swansea of this reorganisation was that the new county council needed a headquarters building, and they chose a site on the Swansea seafront to erect West Glamorgan County Hall. The site had previously been the Paxton Street locomotive depot, along with Sloane Street. The neighbouring Dunvant Place was cleared to make way for the staff and visitors' car park.

1980S AND BEYOND

The major change, and one with greater significance for the prosperity of Swansea and its hinterland, was the creation of the Swansea Enterprise Zone in the Lower Swansea Valley in 1981. The concept of enterprise zones was a new one so, in a sense, the Swansea Enterprise Zone was something of an experiment. There was a debate as to whether the businesses allowed to open there should be manufacturing only, or should there be a mix of manufacturing, retailing and service sector businesses. In the end, the latter view prevailed and all three types of business can be found in the enterprise zone today.

There are two large superstores – Asda and Tesco – plus many smaller retail outlets. Wholesalers can also be found in the zone, along with banks, hotels, accountants, solicitors, financial advisors, cafés, car dealerships, plus the anticipated light industry. The main recycling centre for Swansea can be found here, along with a garden centre and a large lake, which formerly provided water to one of the works that existed here and now has a footpath and trees around it.

A short distance away, to the south, is the Morfa Retail Park, built in the shadow of Brunel's Landore Viaduct. This area is purely intended for retail and residential use. Opposite the shops is the Copper Quarter housing development, and beyond that more new housing on the site once occupied by the Swansea Vale Railway Society. South of this complex is the Liberty Stadium, where Swansea

City Football Club and the Ospreys Rugby Club play their home matches.

In 1989 the conversion of the South Dock into a marina was completed. The surrounding area, formerly filled with dockside buildings, is now full of desirable apartments with some shops and yacht-related services such as ships' chandlers. There are a few restaurants, and one dockside warehouse has been converted into a museum. Originally Swansea Industrial & Maritime Museum, it has now been taken over by the National Museum of Wales, and serves as the National Maritime Museum. Next door is the Swansea Leisure Centre, now bearing the title 'LC2'. This has a large swimming pool, with associated water-activity facilities, squash and badminton courts.

There was another reorganisation of local government in Wales in 1996. This time, the purpose was to create unitary authorities within a single-tier organisational structure. West Glamorgan disappeared, as did Lliw Valley. Two unitary authorities took their place: the City & County of Swansea and the County Borough of Neath Port Talbot. Lliw Valley was divided between them, so that part of the Swansea Valley transferred to Neath Port Talbot, whilst the Gorseinon and Pontardulais areas became part of Swansea. There were proposals for yet another local government reorganisation to take effect in 2020, but these have been shelved for the time being.

Like many post-industrial towns in Britain, the twenty-first century has not been too kind to Swansea. The rapid switch to online shopping has left many of the stores in the town struggling to keep up. Closures are now frequent, and closed shops with 'TO LET' signs are commonplace. Homebase, which has gone from Parc Tawe, and British Home Stores, from Oxford Street, are just two household names that are no longer present.

The Kingsway seems to have been quite badly affected, in part, no doubt, to the seemingly constant roadworks. Firstly, the road was altered to accommodate 'bendy buses', and when they proved impractical efforts were made to restore the road as a main thoroughfare. Now, I understand, the site of the old Oceana nightclub, which before that was the Plaza Cinema, plus part of the Kingsway, is to be rebranded as a 'digital village'.

18

FAMOUS SWANSEA PERSONALITIES

Before concluding this history of Swansea, I think that mention of two native performers who found fame on the world stage, plus one other adopted son of Swansea, is appropriate. Swansea has a long and distinguished literary past, having produced or nurtured many poets, novelists, essayists and reviewers. Included among them must be the novelist Kingsley Amis, and the poet and friend of Dylan Thomas, Vernon Watkins, who was, at one time, considered for the post of Poet Laureate. It is Dylan Thomas who is probably the best known nationally and internationally of Swansea's homegrown literary talent, and therefore I will devote a few lines to him.

DYLAN THOMAS

Dylan Thomas was born in 1914 in the Uplands, Swansea. His birthplace is now open as a museum. He attended Swansea Grammar School, but was not a star pupil and left school at 16 to become a journalist. Whilst a teenager, he wrote, and had published, much of his literary output.

He moved to London in an effort to further his career as a poet and writer, marrying Caitlin Macnamara in 1937

Dylan Thomas, 1914–53, sketch portrait by Alfred Janes.

and then moving to Laugharne in West Wales. His works gained him an appreciative following, and he added radio broadcasts and reading tours to his repertoire. He recorded some of his works on disc. He was also touring in the USA, where he found some fame. It was whilst in the USA on his fourth trip that he fell ill and died in 1953, aged 39.

Thomas was perhaps best known as one of the 'Kardomah Boys' because, with a gang of literary and artistic friends, he frequented the Kardomah Café in Castle Street. Whilst writing this book, I discovered that a girl who also frequented the Kardomah at that time is actually still alive, aged 104. When asked her opinion of Dylan Thomas, whom she knew fairly well, she replied, 'He were a big-headed bugger. Thought a lot of himself. Not all that good a poet either!'

SIR HARRY SECOMBE

Sir Harry Secombe was born in 1921 in St Thomas in Swansea. His secondary education was at Dynevor School in the centre of town. His wartime army service was largely spent in North Africa and Italy. As he had always been a singer, particularly in his local church choir, he joined a concert party and developed a comedy routine to entertain the troops.

Right at the end of the war, he joined with Spike Milligan to form a comedy duo. The duo expanded after the war, joining with Michael Bentine and Peter Sellers to become the Goons. This show proved to be very successful and launched Sir Harry as a comic actor and singer. He appeared in a number of stage musicals, including *Pickwick*. After a period of starring in his own TV shows, he turned to presenting religious programmes such as *Songs of Praise*, *Stars on Sunday* and *Highway*. He was awarded a CBE in 1963 and was knighted in 1981. He died in 2001.

THOMAS BOWDLER

Just briefly, I will mention one other well-known name who resided in Swansea for a large part of his life. Thomas Bowdler, born in Bath, came to Swansea in 1811 to Rhyddings House in the Uplands. His claim to fame is that he censored and sanitised the works of Shakespeare and Edward Gibbons to make them acceptable for family reading. The process became known as bowdlerising, and so he has a permanent presence in the English language.

BIBLIOGRAPHY

Arnold, Arthur, *A Winding Trail* (*Western Mail & Echo*, 1943).

Arthur, Nigel, *Swansea at War: A Pictorial Account 1939–45* (Archive Publications, 1988).

Brookes, Geoff, *Swansea in the 1950s: Ten Years that changed a City* (Amberley Publishing, 2015).

Brookes, Geoff, *A–Z of Swansea* (Amberley Publishing, 2016).

Draisey, Derek, *Swansea & Gower in Victorian & Edwardian Times, Vol One* (Draisey Publishing, 2011).

Gabb, Gerald, *Swansea and its History, Vol One* (Gerald Gabb, 2006).

Gittins, Rob, *Rock & Roll to Paradise: The History of the Mumbles Railway* (Gomer Press, 1982).

Gwynn, D.R., Reynolds, P.R. and Warren, H.R., *A Postal History of Swansea and District* (Swansea Philatelic Society, 1984).

Gwynn, David, *Images of Wales: Sketty* (Tempus Publishing, 2004).

Gwynn, David, *Central Swansea Through Time* (Amberley Publishing, 2013).

Gwynn, David, *Lost Swansea* (Amberley Publishing, 2019).

Lewis, Bernard, *Swansea in the Great War* (Pen & Sword, 2014).

Miskell, Louise, *'Intelligent Town': An Urban History of Swansea, 1780–1855* (University of Wales Press, 2006).

Rogers, W.C., *A Pictorial History of Swansea* (Gomer Press, 1981).

'The Vikings in Wales' in *SA4 Community Magazine* (August 2019).

Thomas, Norman L., *The Story of Swansea's Districts & Villages* (Qualprint, 1969).

Williams, Glanmor (ed.), *Swansea: An Illustrated History* (Christopher Davies, 1991).

ACKNOWLEDGEMENTS

No author can produce a book such as this without the support and patience of their family. I must thank most profusely my lovely wife, Alicia, for all the support she has provided over the year or so that I have been closeted with my computer. Also, I must thank my amazing daughter, Caitlin; my wonderful daughter, Rebecca; and my brilliant son, Steffan, for all the help and support I have received from them. I have to extend my heartfelt appreciation to Brian Prouton for the lovely illustrations that he has produced for me. Also, to Shona Small and Bob Harris for their help and advice. Gail McNulty's help with the section on Dylan Thomas has been invaluable, and I must say thank you to her, too.

INDEX